GUIDE TO
SOCIAL MEDIA

SUSIE BONIFACE

© Haynes Publishing 2018
Published June 2018

A CIP Catalogue record for this book
is available from the British Library.

ISBN: 978 1 78521 229 1

Library of Congress control no. 2018932841

Published by Haynes Publishing,
Sparkford, Yeovil, Somerset BA22 7JJ
Tel: 01963 440635
Int. tel: +44 1963 440635
Website: www.haynes.com

Printed in Malaysia.

Bluffer's Guide®, Bluffer's® and Bluff Your Way®
are registered trademarks.

Series Editor: David Allsop.
Front cover illustration by Alan Capel.

CONTENTS

'I have Social Disease. I have to go out every night. If I stay home one night I start spreading rumours to my dogs.'

Andy Warhol

SOCIAL INTERCOURSE

You will often hear people complain that before the invention of social media, people used to talk. They used to meet in 'normal' ways; there was none of this 'sexting' business; we had friends before Facebook, you know...In fact, what people used to do before social media was socialise using different media: cave paintings, storytelling, gossip, smoke signals, carving initials in trees. Updating your Facebook status about your lunchtime ham sandwich is much the same as prehistoric man leaving a handprint on the cave wall to tell everyone he'd caught a really big bison.

And that's the trick to successfully bluffing your way in the confusingly high-tech world of Internet networking and sharing: realising that it is no different to every other way in which human beings talk to and about one another.

As a species, humans have always wanted to share information – and the reason social networking services are so popular is because they make it easier than ever before. Where once you had to corner someone in the next cave to boast about who you had just snogged, today you can put a picture on Instagram and shout it to the whole world.

While some welcome the mass exchange of information, others mistrust technological developments for fear they make us less human. Charles Dickens, confronted with the development of the telegraph, said: 'Electric communication will never be a substitute for the face of someone who with their soul encourages another person to be brave and true.'

Which ironically is the perfect 140-character length for a tweet (if you lose a full stop).

So when someone wants to complain about social media being the death of proper talking, point out to them that apes grunt, Homo erectus had basic symbolic communication, and Homo sapiens uttered the first words sometime between 30,000 and 100,000 years ago. Remind them that humankind is a storytelling species and is unique in that regard.

In the 1960s, some Californian geeks began linking their computers in what became known as the Internet and in 1982 Britain's Tim Berners-Lee developed a way of navigating it with addresses, links and readable pages – the World Wide Web. At this point, the evolution of human communication sped up exponentially, with email in 1993, blogging shortly after, Facebook launching in 2004 and Twitter in 2006.

Four years later the Internet went into warp drive, when astronaut T.J. Creamer sent a tweet unassisted from the International Space Station in orbit above Earth.

And here we are, in the second decade of the twenty-first century, at the point where any of us can have an online conversation with someone on the other side of the world who we've never met, and simultaneously read the news, share amusing animal pictures, watch porn, and farm jelly beans competitively, all while our boss thinks we're working.

Of course, your boring pals might point out that we're so busy with all these distractions that we merely grunt at our nearest and dearest, which means evolution has advanced so far it's actually gone backwards in time. If they do, you can respond with 'AHA! Social media invented time travel too!' and after that they'll probably give up and leave you alone.

While what we say is the same as it's always been, the way we do it is changing at an alarming rate. From a handful of academic web pages in 1969, there are 1.3 billion websites at the time of writing in 2017. About 3.2 billion people used the Internet as of 2015, more than a billion of them in China. Population penetration varies widely between countries and continents, with 78 per cent of Americans online compared to just 31 per cent of Africans.

And it's not just for youngsters. Some 48 per cent of people aged 65 to 74 use social media; 35 per cent of couples who married in the USA between 2005 and 2012 met via social media; and one in five divorces is blamed on Facebook. In a survey, 1 in 7 Brits said they'd considered divorce because of their partner's use of social media, and 25% said they argued about it every week. This is, increasingly, how we live – online, where there's little privacy, constant data harvesting and ever-lurking trolls.

The pace of change being what it is, this guide will probably be out of date before there's been time to hit 'print'. Perhaps one day people will abandon it entirely and go back to banging rocks together, but until then this book will be your best way of learning how to navigate the ever-changing waters of social media.

Maybe you're one of those people who can't go five minutes without grazing Pinterest. Perhaps you have bought or been given this guide in an attempt to haul you into the daunting mêlée of twenty-first-century communication. Either way, this book will tell you things you don't know, warn you about the perils of online intercourse and arm you with the kind of bite-sized knowledge that will make you sound like an expert with very little effort on your part.

It sets out to conduct you through the main danger zones encountered in discussions about social media and to equip you with the vocabulary and evasive technique that will minimise the risk of being rumbled as a bluffer. It will give you a few easy-to-learn hints and techniques that might even allow you to be accepted as a social media expert of rare ability and experience.

It will give you the tools to impress legions of marvelling listeners with your expertise and insight – without anyone discovering that, until you read this, you probably didn't know the difference between a tweet and a dweet.*

---

*It can mean a tweet sent while drunk, while on a date, or even... ahem... while defecating. Humans, eh?

IT'S A TRIBAL THING

The first thing every bluffer needs to know is that the Internet is tribal. Most people use just one or two social media sites, and presume all others are crap.

If you read the newspapers, which concentrate on celebrity users, stalkers and murderers, social media consists entirely of Facebook and Twitter which are filled with all three.

But any site on which humans share social information online qualifies. Here's a quick rundown of the current giants, the up-and-comers and those so passé they're already in the social media graveyard:

FACEBOOK

Born in 2004 to help American college students 'rate' one another's attractiveness, and already the granddad of social media. These days even your mum's on it. Facebook consists of a network of 'friends' who request access to your page, where you can bore them to death with pictures of your latest holiday or child. Best defined as like being invited to a dinner party – it's increasingly middle-aged, varies from dull to shouty, and the guests are mainly old friends from years ago who make you wonder why you're still talking to them. You might hook up with an old school sweetheart or you might realise the object of your unrequited teenage lust became an ignorant chubster.

BLUFFER'S TIP *For that reason alone, it might be a good idea to move to China, where this classic example of the tool of the running-dog capitalist bourgeoisie has been banned since 2009 after independence protesters used it to communicate.*

TWITTER

At the time of writing this is the king of social media, so by the time of publication it could be dead and buried under social media's back porch. Social media is that fast. And so is Twitter, which every bluffer needs to know is officially a 'microblogging' site. When it began every user could write posts limited to 140 characters, which led to a lot of grammatical and spelling innovation. The limit has now been extended to 280 for most tweeters, but it's rarely used and frowned upon by purists. You can make your account private, but if privacy is what you want, you should be on Facebook. Twitter is like a bustling pub – half the people are drunk, you can interact with whomever you choose, and if a famous person talks to you, it's AMAZING.

You can see the posts of whoever you choose to 'follow', so if anyone says Twitter is boring, it's because they are following boring people.Most bluffers know singer Katy

Perry is the most followed person (at the time of writing), with 108 million-odd people hanging on her every word; a good bluffer knows she calls them 'Katycats'; and a really excellent bluffer can point out she only follows 207 people (again correct at the time of writing), so is presumably more interested in broadcasting than listening.

BLUFFER'S TIP *Talk confidently about Twitter's peculiar ability to lose money for its parent company compared to the Facebook cash juggernaut, which is due to fewer users and even fewer adverts. Twitter v Facebook is socialism v capitalism, and humans are the commodity.*

REDDIT

A huge bulletin board where registered users called Redditors submit posts or links, which are then voted up or down the newsfeed according to their popularity. Founded, as so many sites are, by university students, it was snapped up by the owners of Condé Nast publishing in 2011 for under $20 million and is now worth an estimated $1.8 billion. The founders returned a few years later when it had an issue with trolling, and now Reddit has 250 million active users – a bigger population than Brazil.

Different to other sites in that all posts are categorised, first labelled for example as 'education' or 'image sharing', and then with 5,400 further detailed tags within those categories known as 'subreddits'. For example, the education category has subreddits for movies, gaming, music and 'creepy', which is a place you are advised to enter with caution.

BLUFFER'S TIP *The most popular and newsworthy bit of Reddit is AMA – Ask Me Anything. It's where a person can be asked literally any question, and everyone else can follow the thread of their replies to the community. The most popular AMAs have been done by Barack Obama, Madonna and George Clooney; celebrities who refuse to answer questions unrelated to whatever they're promoting get a bad reaction.*

The best AMA ever was the anonymous user called Double Dick Dude, who started his session off saying: 'I am the guy with two penises. Ask me anything.' Educational AND creepy.

LINKEDIN

An online Rolodex, and about as much fun. Used by 'professionals' to 'connect' with 'networkers' and post their CVs. Makes money with subscription-only recruitment tools, so employers can hunt down the right candidate and agencies can harass people who've forgotten they joined it. Many of its 467 million users have long since marked its twice-daily 'invitations to connect' emails as spam and realised it's not a good place to post photographs of the night that was lost to tequila. Despite that, it's a networking behemoth that Microsoft spent $26 billion on in 2016 and taken very seriously by people who are very serious. Not enough fun to be blocked in China.

BLUFFER'S TIP *Don't join. Your dad's on it.*

INSTAGRAM

Wildly popular method of taking a photograph of yourself, digitally enhancing it so you look hot, then posting it online with a smug comment about how crazy/fun/cool you are. Populated by celebrities like Kim Kardashian and the members of One Direction, as well as newspaper journalists who can rip the pictures down and use them without fear of copyright infringement. Bought by Facebook for $1 billion in 2012 when it had 30 million users, it had grown to 800 million users by the end of 2017. That means one third of ALL Internet users in the world are on this site, where they post 95 million pictures a DAY. Social media began eating itself when 'Rich Kids of Instagram', with pictures of daddy's helicopter, skiing holidays and Cristal-laced proms, stopped being a piss-take on Instagram and got its own entirely-serious Tumblr (*see* next page).

'It is said that if you know your enemies and know yourself, you will not be imperilled in a hundred battles.'

Sun Tzu

Do say 'Did you know 68 per cent of Instagrammers are female?'

Don't say 'God, the paparazzi are awful. Here are some of my holiday snaps.'

YOUTUBE

Responsible for Justin Bieber, which is good enough reason to call for its immediate global ban. In the meantime, it's a way of sharing videos, exploited not just by TV types, but also by anyone with something to market – in Bieber's case, his singing. In 2007, his mum uploaded a video of him singing at school and kept doing it. He built up a fan base, was discovered by a manager, introduced to Usher, and was launched into hyperfame. You can set up your own 'channel', subscribe to channels you like, and post comments which vary from 'LOVE THIS!' to 'U so fat.' Criticised widely for its content, which can include porn, Arab Spring disputes, jihadist beheadings and explanations about what's inside your laptop and how to replace the screen. Also home to every half-amusing cat video on Earth.

BLUFFER'S TIP *Can be surprisingly useful, especially if you need to replace your laptop screen.*

TUMBLR

A blogging site which encourages people to use pictures and as few words as possible. A Tumblr might be a collection of videos of George Osborne's girly hands, a series of pretend conversations with your dog, or a thoughtful study of the British love of queuing. A few minutes on Tumblr leaves you with the feel and look of mild sedation. Texts From Dog – a Tumblr featuring mocked-up iPhone messages from, yes, a dog – was so popular it became a book. In

August 2015 Tumblr's users were uploading 75 million posts a day. A sizeable chunk are pornographic.

BLUFFER'S TIP *Stay off it if you want to achieve anything with your life.*

PINTEREST

A bit like Tumblr, but you add your pictures to a pinboard in any one of a number of categories, so all of your 'my beautiful baby' photos are in one place and other people don't have to look at them if they don't want to. You can follow boards, set up new ones, post pictures to different boards, but this is fundamentally Pictures Only I Am Interested In.

BLUFFER'S TIP *It's filled with pedants complaining that your arty picture of cinnamon sticks doesn't belong on a board about ground spices.*

GOOGLE+

Basically, The Matrix. Everything you do online – searches, blogs, videos, email, photos – get linked together and have your name put on them. Great for megalomaniacs and businesses, bothersome for individuals who don't like Google's total domination of the multiverse. If you join, you'll need Laurence Fishburne to get you out again.

BLUFFER'S TIP *If you're tempted to join Google+, reach behind your head, pull out the cable connecting you to the robots' mainframe, and escape.*

SNAPCHAT

An app which allows users to send messages, pictures or videos available to the recipient for between one and 10 seconds, after which it seems to disappear from your device. By the end of 2017 it was being used to send 3 billion Snaps a day by 173 million users, and went public the same year at $29 billion. Shares dipped but investors are holding on because the site boasts 30% of all US millennials.

BLUFFER'S TIP *Some will claim Snapchat is used by teenagers to sext one another, attracted by the fact that saucy pictures are instantly deleted. While most of its users are aged 13 to 23, less than 15 per cent of them admit to ever using it for sexy times; instead most, 60 per cent, say they use it to send 'funny faces'. Oh, and for a superbluff, point out that Snaps can be retrieved with minimal technical knowledge on your device and remain forever on the Snapchat servers.*

WHATSAPP

Instant messaging service where subscribers can talk to each other for free – circumventing pricey text and picture messaging, and also enabling you to send messages to a group of contacts. Bought by Facebook for $19 billion and with a billion active users as of 2017, it was criticised for being too open to hackers so it decided to encrypt all messages, which in turn meant it was criticised by governments worldwide for being unhackable and therefore a safe haven for terrorists. Goes to show, you just can't win.

A respectful silence now as bluffers pause to consider the social media sites that are either dead, dying or gravely ill.

MYSPACE

Social media with music, bought by Rupert Murdoch for half a billion dollars just two years after it launched back in 2003. He later sold it to a partnership including Justin Timberlake. Used to be a great place to find new bands; now moribund and populated by teenagers who want to 'make it big' and *X Factor* production assistants promising the world if you'll just come on TV to be humiliated. It's the Casio keyboard of the twenty-first century.

BLUFFER'S TIP *If asked about MySpace, you must be too cool to have ever known about it. The correct bluff is to screw up your face, look confused, and say 'Huh?'*

BEBO

This was basically a profile page where you could post quizzes, photos, videos or blogs. Set up by a Brit in 2005, it smashed MySpace, was sold for $850 million to AOL in 2008, got overtaken by Facebook, went phut, and was bought back by the original owners for $1 million. It was shut pending a relaunch, which turned out to be reinvention as a company making social apps for others. Its first app, Blab, launched in 2014 and closed two years later.

Don't spend Any money on it whatsoever.

Do say 'Bebo? Deader than disco.'

BLUFFER'S TIP *If you set up a social media website, sell it as early as possible.*

VINE

A video service where users post looping six-second video clips and can upload them to Twitter or Facebook. It began in June 2012 and was sold an astonishing four months later to Twitter for a reported $970 million, and has since been used to document the aftermath of the bombing of the US Embassy in Ankara, criticise actor Ryan Gosling for not eating his cereal, and it even got obscure twerking song 'Don't Drop That Thun Thun' to number 35 on the US music chart. It was discontinued in 2016, making it one of the more short-lived examples of how to waste a billion dollars.

BLUFFER'S TIP *Be aware that Vine is the reason the UK was introduced to controversial 'comedian' Dapper Laughs, a former estate agent called Daniel O'Reilly who posted what he claimed were character-based sexist rants about women – 'she wants it' and so on – and got a TV show on the back of it. The show was cancelled after he made jokes about rape, thus proving that what might seem funny in the privacy of your smartphone is less amusing in the living room in front of your mum.*

PERISCOPE, MEERKAT, LIVESTREAM

A series of broadcasting apps, allowing users to upload live video. Useful to witness live events perhaps, but a minefield for privacy and piracy issues – particularly at pay-per-view sports events, cinemas, or if used to peek at someone who doesn't know you're doing it.

The trolling was atrocious due to anonymous comments. These days Periscope doesn't like talking about how many users it does (not) have, Meerkat was shut down in 2016, and only Livestream is still with us – perhaps because it went subscription-only in 2016.

FOURSQUARE

A method for combining geography and smugness and multiplying it by one-upmanship. You used to get a notification when users 'check in' at venues, i.e., 'Sam checked in at the Cutest Bakery Ever', 'Sam checked in at Trump Tower', 'Sam checked in at GirlzGirlzGirlz and then quickly deleted it'. In 2014 Microsoft spent $15 million on it to harvest data about user habits for targeted marketing purposes. These days it's a local search and discovery app, allowing people to swap reviews of places they've been.

BLUFFER'S TIP *If the product is free, you are the thing on sale.*

LAST FM

This records which tracks you listen to online. Users can network, get info about bands and get recommendations. Basically a way of letting the whole world know you're the last person still listening to Mel and Kim.

BLUFFER'S TIP *When asked about Last FM, say: 'Can't you make up your own mind about what to listen to? LOSER.'*

FRIENDS REUNITED

Launched in 2000 as a way of spying on old school friends, it once had 19 million users. It now has a lot fewer, and a place in the history books. Owned by the Dundee publisher of *The Beano*, it is today used mainly by grannies that want to know 'how this Internet thing works'.

BLUFFER'S TIP *Say you're too young to remember it.*

But that's not all. Aside from the websites and apps you can use on an individual basis with your own page and your own little network of people who might be interested in it, there are a bunch of social media sites that are more of a team effort.

Blogger and Wordpress both provide you with the tools to build your own blog (short for web log) by laying out a page, getting an unique web address or URL, editing the format and so on. But there are so many people using them that they have become a social network on their own. Blogger has 46 million of them, Wordpress 75 million, and Tumblr – which is 'microblogging' – boasts 350 million. It's possible to do nothing but cruise blogs all day, linking them to your own, commenting on theirs, and obviously wincing at daylight and sudden noises.

Then there are sites which aggregate their content. Some bright spark starts up their own page, and adds other people's work to it. Some sites aggregate news, like the Drudge Report which finds the best stories on newspaper websites, repackages them slightly and links out to the original content. Others aggregate blogs, like

Mumsnet, which hosts the blogs of those who want to join and highlights a select few, massively increasing the audience of those lucky enough to be chosen.

Sites aggregate polls, videos, the best animal GIFs, car insurance offers, anything. And there are even apps and sites that let you aggregate your social media, after someone worked out that users normally use more than one and there's a lot of overlap. Eventually there'll be ways of aggregating the aggregators, and when that day dawns it's time to turn the computer off and go outside for some fresh air.

There are also collaborations, when a random bunch of users combine their efforts to create something. A prime example is Wikipedia, a free online encyclopedia where registered users can add and edit entries on everything from the biographical details of Bill Clinton's love affairs to an analysis of Mao Tse-tung's military strategy. It's basically a 'hive mind' to dip into and you can frequently find the right answer, but as editing can be done by anyone it's easy to get caught out – partly because Wikipedia always sounds believable and partly because the Internet is filled with people who like pranks and getting drunk.

Celebrities are prime targets, with journalists frequently repeating claims they have died, once dated Liz Taylor or said something they didn't. Hoaxes include a 4,500-word entirely fictitious article on the Bicholim conflict of India, which never happened but remained online for five years – an achievement any bluffer would be proud of. Award-winning British journalist Johann Hari was disgraced after it was found he used a pseudonym to alter his own Wiki page and edit the pages of his enemies.

Cynics know it as 'Nickitpedia' because it's so easy to cut-and-paste supposed facts – and even Sir Brian Leveson was caught out when his report of a two-year inquiry into press practices quoted *The Independent* newspaper's Wikipedia page. Unbeknown to Brian, a 25-year-old Californian called Brett Straub was not a founder of that august organ. And unbeknown to Brett, a mate of his had added his name to the page for a laugh.

You know you've made it in social media bluffing if you can not only figure out how to edit a Wikipedia page, but then find that edit later stated as fact in the *Daily Mail*.

Game worlds also qualify as social networks – sites like Second Life where users adopt a persona and build a whole online existence, battling demons or falling in love and even running profitable businesses. Do not get involved with one unless you want to become morbidly fascinated with things that aren't real, and always remember the cautionary tale of Dave Pollard and Amy Taylor.

Their online avatars met in an Internet chatroom in 2003 and got married in Second Life in 2005. In 2008 it was reported Amy discovered Dave on his computer watching his avatar having cybersex with an avatar operated by Linda Brinkley, and demanded a divorce.

Needless to say, in reality they all looked a little different to their avatars, and made even less sense. A wise bluffer avoids this sort of thing – there is no way to successfully bluff someone who lives, quite literally, in a different world. In the words of William Shatner in a *Saturday Night Live* sketch set at a *Star Trek* convention: 'Get a life!'

USERS AND ABUSERS

If social media is a party, it's one that Paris Hilton would have left already.

Since its geeky origins in the computer departments of American college campuses, Internet users have been derided as unwashed, afraid of daylight, and socially inept.

There are a lot of people like that. But consisting as they do of human beings, the users (and abusers) of social media are a varied bunch.

Given that your aim as a bluffer will be to impress them, here are the main types to watch out for and how to handle them:

TROLLS

Known to the scientific community as 'sociopaths', trolls are users who in simple terms want attention and do exactly what any toddler would do to get it – hurl their nappy.

They might post 'LOL GLAD SHE'S DEAD' on a

Facebook page memorialising a recently deceased teen; they may tweet rape threats to female celebrities or politicians; or issue death threats that seem eerily credible when they know where you were because you tagged your location on Instagram.

> 'I don't like parties past 2am.
> Then it's all losers and weirdos.'
> *Paris Hilton*

Because you can't see them, trolls are often presumed to be sentient beings capable of causing the harm they wish upon others. However, as increasingly frequent prosecutions and trips to court have proven, there has never yet been a troll who had a healthy mental attitude, steady job or the requisite literacy to locate anyone's home address with any accuracy.

They also all look like they were left behind in the field when people were picking the best-looking Cabbage Patch dolls.

The preferred method for dealing with them is to ignore, block and, in extreme cases, report to the police who will generally ignore them for you. Never, ever, respond unless it's to correct their abuse for punctuation and spelling. And never, ever, be tempted to turn up on THEIR doorstep with a newly purchased and invitingly gleaming axe.

THE EASILY OUTRAGED

The sort who cannot see a bandwagon without jumping on it. Whatever is trending, whatever is 'most read', this person will be REALLY upset about it. The *Daily Mirror*'s latest front page, the government's new policy, what Madonna said to Lady Gaga, OMG did you see that homophobic tweet from Vladimir Putin? These people want to feel included, so share in the outrage of others while propagating it by resharing the outrage on all of their social media sites so everyone else can be upset. They are completely immune to logic, with a typical insult being along the lines of: 'You right-wing, liberal, tea-drinking, metropolitan-county dwelling elitist peasant scum!' Bear in mind that their ultimate ambition is to be quoted in a national newspaper after the phrase, 'People took to Twitter to say…'

PEOPLE PRETENDING TO BE SOMEONE THEY'RE NOT

There are, at the last count, around 330 million Twitter accounts in the world. Maths tells us that must be around one in every 23 people on the planet – and common sense tells us that can't be right. That's because there are lots of people who have more than one online identity.

Some tweet as their own dog or cat, which is sort of sweet for five minutes. Some tweet as God, or the

Queen, others as a cake-obsessed Henry VIII, fictional TV characters, MPs, and one enterprising if deluded soul maintains an online presence as Stephen Fry's wife. Their aim is to be funny, get a book deal and achieve recognition for their wit/insight/satire. They are easily impressed by a fictitious persona with more followers than them, and they are terrified of being diagnosed with multiple-personality disorder.

THE PROLIFIC USER

Has an account on every social network, knows all the gossip, and has linked their media so that whatever they type on one website is simultaneously regurgitated on all others. Likely to use online phrases such as 'LOL' and 'hmm, Pinteresting…' in everyday conversation, wear skinny jeans and have a bad haircut. Constantly worries about 'what's happening online', sleeps with their smartphone by their bed, rarely eats properly, never has sex (unless it's with themselves), and if they do they're checking their notifications before, during and after. They are easily impressed by an acronym they've never heard of.

THE OVERSHARER

Often a new parent, but just as likely to be anyone who wants to tell everyone they know and lots of people they don't know just how AMAZING or AWFUL their life is on a six-times-daily basis. If it's not pictures of what Little Tabitha is up to, it's a rundown of their smear test or prostate exam, commuting commentary or a detailed description of their dinner. Positive or negative, this person is generally unbearable but so desperate for acceptance they will know instantly if you dissociate yourself from their updates. 'Why did you unfriend me?' 'Don't you like me?' 'How can't you share my anguish that the local sewer has overflowed and I've got turds bobbing around my kitchen?', etc. Can be defeated only by bombarding them with your own constant dull updates, but beware, if you do this you could get sucked in.

They are invariably impressed by someone whose life is just like theirs, only better. They live in fear of being deleted.

THE DINOSAUR

Someone who has decided they ought to figure out this social media thing and can't. Whether for work or to keep an eye on their partner/offspring, they sign up to a site without any idea of the unwritten rules. They can't find their privacy settings, their one tweet reads 'How does this work?' and they're only online twice a year in case someone steals their identity. They are perplexed as to how anyone can make 'the Internet' a job.

However, do not misjudge The Dinosaur. They are guaranteed to be the one person who sees that unfortunate picture of you playing Neknominate (*see* 'Crazes', page 82) in a mankini and tells your family all about it. They also take no prisoners when dealing with trolls, largely because they believe them to be mythical.

They are impressed by everything (especially Instagram picture filters) and terrified by all of it.

THE ENTREPRENEUR

The precise opposite of The Dinosaur, they know and understand social media and have made it work for them. It could be by designing apps and games, setting up a blog which went global, or establishing a website flogging stuff and marketing it online. In all likelihood, they are a millionaire or billionaire before the age of 25, and even more likely to have done it from their teenage bedroom when they should have been doing their homework. Will be carrying the latest smartphone, talk in computer code and still be suffering from acne.

Their role models are Bill Gates, Steve Jobs and Mark Zuckerberg. They live in dread of a lack of Wi-Fi.

SEX PESTS

Well, obviously. This is humankind, remember, and they wrongly think they're anonymous and untraceable online. On most social media, you can expect to be spammed by fraudsters offering marriage with a Russian lady or counterfeit Viagra, but they are at least trying to make a business out of it. You will also find random approaches from people pretending to be the next Messiah, or celebrities, or politicians (actually they're not pretending), and how they'd like to hook up or send you photographs of their naughty bits. When this happens, screenshot their sleaze and publish it – social media means that we all get to share, and shame is a powerful deterrent to further perving. And if they're famous, newspapers pay good money for that sort of thing.

COMMENTERS

Comments are what makes social media – it's an exchange of reactions to whatever is being commented upon, be it a status update, tweet, blog, video or picture. Many use comments to interact and to modify their own opinion, but truly dedicated commenters want to force their world view on others. They might think they're telling truth unto power, coming up with witty satire, reliving the Second World War, or stopping the spread of society-destroying gay sex/socialism/poor grammar. They're the sort of people who are likely to say 'I'm not a racist, but…' or 'Isn't this how Nazi Germany started?', while adding a link to their own, little-read blog or opinion in the hope of attracting two more visitors. The kind of person who finds it hard to go to bed when they think someone on the Internet is wrong, and therefore dwells in the twilight world of those driven mildly insane by sleep deprivation.

They are sure to be impressed by anyone who can link the Austro-Hungarian alliance of 1879 and global warming in one pithy paragraph. And they live in terror of moderators deleting their remarks.

BLOGGERS

Blogs are basically online diaries, which means bloggers are all the sort of people prepared to let others read their diary. Some are personal, others support a business or are trying to sell a book, and some are hired to make other people's websites more interesting. Some are very niche (blogs about embroidery tips), others more general (blogs about celebrity gossip), some purely capitalist (blogs about 'how to make money from blogging' courses – £400 a head). They are all, fundamentally, laying themselves bare and hoping others like what they see in the greater hope that they might pay for it. It's basically a red light district for those with a keyboard. They are most impressed by 'unique user statistics', which is the number of people who visit a site or read a blog.

Bloggers live in mortal fear of lawsuits or accidentally deleting their unpublished novel.

LURKERS

These people sign up to social media, follow, befriend and watch everyone else, while at no point talking to anyone. Either painfully shy or just plain stalkers, they like to be at the party and know what everyone is doing at the party, but not in any way be the person dancing on the table at the party. They're part of a strange Internet netherworld where they click, they laugh, they hate, they unfriend, and no one ever knows they were there.

They are impressed by fame, yet terrified of being noticed.

PEOPLE WHO HAVE FORGOTTEN WHAT THEY ARE SUPPOSED TO BE DOING

It's 3pm, they're stuck on a '23 ways cats are like biscuits' page of GIFs, and look like they've been heavily sedated.

They are always impressed by a better cat video, and are terrified by actual cats.

'I have ways of making money that you know nothing of.'

John D. Rockefeller

CYBERBUCKS

Social media is not just a way of wasting your time and atrophying vital motor functions – for an increasing number of people it has turned into something approaching a proper job.

From billion-dollar stock flotations to phone apps that make some geeks $50,000 a day to YouTube celebrities, social media is one big moneymaking opportunity for those who know how to milk it.

We're not talking about that elusive Lithuanian lady who says she loves you and wants your bank details to come and stay for a week. She's pretty enterprising, but the true social media millionaires make her look about as motivated as a sloth.

A world-class bluffer will need to know not only the ways you can make money online, but also the players, revenues and biggest yarns involved in doing exactly that.

A quick Google search for 'make money online' will pull up 67,100,000 pages suggesting you bank your sperm, sell breast milk, or even answer Internet surveys for anything from a few pennies to a few pounds at a time.

Most of us have sold off unwanted things from the attic on eBay, found a bargain on a website at half the price on the High Street, or in some other way made a bit of cash from the Internet.

But that's all small fry compared to some of the truly big moneymaking beasts of social media.

Probably the most famous is Mark Zuckerberg, the gawky kid who started Facebook with university friends and has since been the subject of a massive lawsuit, a Hollywood movie, and all the attention that comes with being worth an estimated $72.3 billion.

Bluffers need to know that Facebook's stock market float in 2012 was the biggest tech float of all time and valued the site at $100 billion – that's $31 a share.

After trading began, values immediately plummeted, causing critics to talk about the second dot-com bubble and point out that a free-to-use website was a silly business plan.

But those who held their nerve are laughing now, because the shares are worth nearly five times what they were at float and Facebook is so rich it spends billions gobbling up other social networks.

There are companies set up and run within Facebook as well – firms which exist purely to advertise and trade to Facebook users, selling clothes, shoes, music – basically anything your profile's 'likes' and interactions tell the developers you'd be interested in.

There are also – naturally – companies which, for a fee, will provide a few thousand more 'likes' for your company's Facebook profile, falsely increasing its popularity.

It's commonly said online that if you're not paying, then you're the product, and nothing could be truer of Facebook. Once you sign up, they simply collect data and use it to work out what they can sell you.

They even know how long your relationship is likely to last, depending on when and how you change your 'relationship status'.

And yes, people willingly sign up to all this darkness because it's free and they want to know just how minging their high school sweetheart looks now.

Zuckerberg might be a billionaire, but he generally wears flip-flops in public and lives in a $3 million, five-bed house in Silicon Valley where his main indulgence seems to be the fact that he dropped another $30 million to buy four neighbouring houses at well over their market value to protect his privacy.

Not all Internet entrepreneurs live so quietly. Twitter chairman Jack Dorsey spends his $2.8 billion in a more lively fashion, and has been seen holidaying on his yacht with supermodel Lily Cole.

Mark Cuban, a former bartender who found a way to stream radio sports commentary online, made $5.7 billion from selling Broadcast.com to Yahoo! in 1999. Broadcast has stopped broadcasting, but Mr Cuban has used the cash wisely, buying a basketball team and a cable TV network, and offering Donald Trump $1m to shave his head.

Then you have the likes of Jimmy Wales, the founder

of not-for-profit Wikipedia which is the fifth-most-visited website on the planet.

A former university teacher and finance worker, he has an $85 Chinese phone and a personal net worth – that's including house, shares, salary – of just $1 million. It's thought Wikipedia could be worth $5 billion if he allowed adverts, but he won't. Good for him.

However, he's not all hippy-dippy-who-needs-money-anyway. A good bluffer will know that Wikipedia was founded using money from an earlier venture of Jimmy Wales's called Bomis, which specialised in X-rated content.

Then there are people who manage, by way of the Internet, to make themselves into something they could never otherwise hope to be.

Perez Hilton started out in life as Mario Lavandeira Jr, and worked as an actor, receptionist and freelance writer. He started blogging about celebrities 'because it seemed easy' and posted paparazzi pictures with snarky remarks scrawled over them, outing privately gay stars and generally being as bitchy as hell.

Within six months, it was Hollywood's most hated website. He falsely reported Fidel Castro's death, posted a picture taken up Miley Cyrus' skirt while she was underage, and became known for malicious commentary. PerezHilton.com is worth millions, and Perez has made himself that thing he writes about – a celebrity.

Pete Cashmore took a different route. As a 19-year-old working in his bedroom at home in Banchory, Aberdeen, he set up a blog called Mashable, reporting the latest tech and social media developments. It started out plain and worthy, but with a few layout and design tweaks, it was getting millions of readers a month.

The first his parents knew about it was when a *Daily Mail* reporter knocked on their door asking to speak to the Internet wunderkind upstairs. Mashable hit 45 million monthly users in 2015 and Cashmore, now 32, was named one of *Time* magazine's 100 most influential people. Mashable was sold for $50 million in 2017.

There are also opportunities for people who can't write computer code or set up websites, and these include being paid to write blogs or tweet for other people. Some businesses are desperate to generate customers on social media, but can't be bothered to go to the effort of understanding it for themselves.

This is where someone who can grasp the basics can bluff their way into a reasonably steady job from an employer who is impressed by anyone who can tell a ROFLCOPTER from a LOL (see glossary).

Any medium-rate bluffer should be able to manage it, but beware – even the truly Internet-ignorant might be able to catch you out.

Be aware when applying for any job that even the most prehistoric manager will Google you and will, in all likelihood, be more than horrified to find an open Facebook page featuring pictures of you in a state of undress, or tweets depicting your attempt to down a cocktail of sherry and lighter fuel while standing on the roof in your nan's nightie.

When going for any job, Internet-based or otherwise, it's best to check your social media so that nothing embarrassing can crop up in the interview. This is doubly important if pitching yourself as some sort of Internet expert.

One sure-fire way of guaranteeing to either impress or confuse your interviewer is to send them your CV by way of YouTube. These are called 'Me-Vees', for bluffers who need to know the terminology, and 85 per cent of young people in a recent survey thought they were a good way to show prospective employers what your personality was like.

On the one hand, this can be a more impressive, attention-grabbing way of proving to a prospective boss that you're clean, articulate, attractive and tech-savvy. But it can go horribly wrong.

In October 2006, Yale University student Aleksey Vayner applied for a job with investment bank UBS using a seven-minute video CV. In it, he boasted 'impossible is nothing', and was seen talking about how brilliant he was while skiing, bench-pressing, playing tennis, Latin dancing and finally karate-chopping a stack of seven bricks.

Someone at UBS thought it was hysterical and forwarded it to friends. The video went viral, was mocked by millions, and Aleksey said he hit 'rock bottom'.

He changed his name to Alex Stone to escape the notoriety and launched legal actions against websites hosting the video, with little success.

He was later found to have also claimed that he ran a hedge fund which did not exist, that the Dalai Lama wrote his college application letter, and that he once forged passports for the Russian mafia.

Sadly for his family, Aleksey died in 2013 of a suspected overdose aged just 29, making many people wonder whether social media had killed a modern video star.

Fittingly perhaps, news of his death broke and was spread online – which takes us neatly into the next chapter, on how social media has changed our news forever.

'The paramedic called the press and sold me like a loaf of bread. This was news, and he wanted to be the one to report it.'

Charlie Sheen

TWEET THE TRUTH AND SHAME THE DEVIL

Oh, Charlie. There's no one who has 'Whathafu?' stamped across their forehead quite like a celebrity who live-tweets their drugs-and-hooker benders and then complains about a lack of privacy.

Mr Sheen (the actor, not the furniture polish) does have a point though. Thanks to social media, everyone everywhere is not only a reporter but also an editor, publisher and snarky columnist with a point to make.

The paramedic who leaked details of Charlie's intoxication didn't need to ring the press – he could have tweeted, Facebooked or Instagrammed a picture on his smartphone saying 'HEY LOOK EVERY1 CHARLIE SHEEN IS STONED!' and it would have gone around the world in less time than it takes for the Sheen lawyers to get their boots on.

This is something that causes great irritation both to the famous, who find themselves besieged by wannabe paparazzi at every turn, and the not-famous, who find the definition of 'news' has changed.

It used to be a healthy mix of man-bites-dog and dog-bites-man; these days it's more like a celebrity-filled outrage bus on a whistle-stop tour of the world's worst asylums.

Imagine one of the nation's favourite people telling us what he had for dinner, and what might happen as a result:

'@stephenfry: Eating lovely fresh bananas with some good chums. Hope you're all well!'

'OMG @stephenfry'

'This is not why I follow you. Have you nothing to say about the lack of basic rights for fruit who do not choose to be eaten? #wakeupsheeple #bananafreedom'

'Hey @stephenfry YOU FRUITY or wot?'

'Please sign my epetition about reducing the carbon footprint of fruit imports here…'

'Hello @stephenfry I'm a reporter for the Daily Gullet. We've done a story on the fact your bananas created 346 tonnes of carbon dioxide and four outraged tweets. Any comment? Ta x'

Suddenly, and with enough social media welly behind it in the shape of shares, retweets and reaction, Stephen Fry's dinner choices become news. Do we care what he eats? Not really, but suddenly we're all talking about it even if only to say that we're not interested.

And of course, journalists get a cheap and easy story that the celebrity is unable to deny.

There's an upside to all this so-called citizen journalism – which is that sometimes what catches the mood on social media really IS news.

On 30 June 2007, two men packed a Jeep Cherokee with propane canisters and smashed it into the glass doors of the main terminal at Glasgow Airport.

Both were arrested at the scene, one severely burnt, and five bystanders were injured. Emergency services rushed to put out the blaze and as word spread, 'ordinary' journalists were dispatched to get the story.

The problem was that the authorities had thrown a security cordon around the airport, and no one was getting in or out.

The incident happened at 3pm – just in time to rewrite the next day's papers – but reporters could not find eyewitnesses, photographers couldn't get shots and there was no way to find out what was going on before deadline. Editors were panicking and then one bright spark realised it was all over the Internet. People inside the airport terminal were contacting relatives to let them know they were okay, posting pictures and telling others what had happened.

Suddenly an empty newspaper could be filled with

eyewitness accounts, images of the blazing car, and human interest stories like that of heroic baggage handler John Smeaton who was said to have shouted, 'F***in' c'mon, then', as he launched a flying kick at one of the terrorists.

The story led the news for days and Smeaton got the Queen's Gallantry Medal. Seven others also won bravery awards – they probably wouldn't have done if the citizens who witnessed their actions had not told the story on social media.

Two years later came an event that defined Twitter in particular as a medium for making and breaking news.

Latvian émigré Janis Krums, 23, was on a New York commuter ferry when US Airways flight 1549 ditched in the freezing cold Hudson River. Both engines had been knocked out by a bird strike, and as the plane lost height and power over a crowded metropolitan area, the captain had no choice but to try to glide the plane in over water.

Amazingly, all 155 passengers survived, and the whole drama was captured by CCTV and camera phones, and had more eyewitnesses than you could shake a stick at.

Janis's boat was the first to reach the stranded plane to begin rescuing passengers, and he took a photo of it on his smartphone.

He uploaded it to Twitter, saying, 'There's a plane in the Hudson. I'm on the ferry going to pick up the people. Crazy.'

It's a shame he couldn't come up with something

more pithy and meaningful, because even though he had only 170 followers, within minutes that picture had gone around the world and had become the iconic image of what became known as 'The Miracle On The Hudson'.

Janis said afterwards: 'I had no idea that it would do what it did. I actually gave my phone to one of the passengers that we rescued. Once I got the phone back, I started to get text messages and calls from what seemed like every news outlet.'

Janis's picture led the front page of almost every newspaper in the world next day, and he was interviewed on dozens of TV news channels. His 170 followers jumped to 10,000 and he ended up launching his own recruitment website off the back of his newfound reputation as an Internet expert.

He didn't get paid by most people who used his iconic image. That's the other thing about the Internet – people expect it to be free, when doing it well costs money.

Few news organisations can get their chief executives' heads around this knotty problem. Instead, they gaze longingly at sites like Buzzfeed, which started off providing entertainment in bite-size pieces and did so well that it now provides news in similar-sized pieces. It wouldn't exist without social media, which is how it is spread and read.

Rather than the 600-word articles you might find on a news website, Buzzfeed has snappy picture-driven and easily-digested snippets, that for example take a story covered by a newspaper, boil it down to three paragraphs, and add 16 pictures and a funny flow chart.

The Buzzfeed front page could boast articles such as '31 April Fool's Day Gags Your Mum Will Fall For', '14 Ways That Celebrity Marriage Breakdowns Are Better Than Normal Marriage Breakdowns' and 'Tony Blair – What Does A Peace Envoy Do? [With GIFs]'.

The site has been accused of stealing content from others, and in 2017 it was reported that up to 45 people at its UK office – a third of the British staff – would be laid off amid talk of a digital advertising slowdown.

The rest of the world, meanwhile, is using social media for other stuff. Take for example the revolutionary wave of protests and demonstrations that spread across the Middle East in 2010 and 2011 and became known as the Arab Spring.

Activists and bystanders posted videos, pictures and commentary online and made it possible for the rest of the world to see what was happening in Tunisia, Egypt and Bahrain, among others. Foreign news organisations could report on it, international pressure was put upon the leaders scrutinised while ruthlessly quashing demonstrations, and several governments fell pretty peacefully as a result.

It didn't work everywhere – Libya had foreign military intervention and is now home to terror training camps and a fractured, cobbled-together government. Syria has had a civil war lasting years and displacing millions. All sides in that conflict use social media to show what their nasty enemies are up to/report their own glorious victories, and jihadist factions use

YouTube to both recruit new soldiers and demonstrate to their financial backers what the grenades are being used for.

And therein lies the problem with 'citizen journalism' – which is that the cameras often lie, and so do the reporters.

'I wake up in the morning, and I make my hairbow, and I put my cat suit on, and I call up everybody in the Haus of Gaga, and I say, "How are we gonna be brilliant today?"'

Lady Gaga

BECOMING A SOCIAL MEDIA MONSTER

The pop star Lady Gaga – real name Stefani Germanotta – is a clever woman.

Not only did she take everything Madonna and David Bowie ever did and do it again with very few changes to give herself worldwide superstardom and a net worth of somewhere over £205 million, she also knows – somewhere, deep inside, beyond the post-ironic remarks in her lyrics – that she is actually a monster.

Monsters, by definition, are frightening and daunting things of unusual size, possibly unpleasant, but always odd. It's usually taken to mean you have snakes for hair, the hind legs of a goat – that sort of thing.

In the world of social media, monsters are the ones who get very big, very quickly, then find themselves unable to be anything else. Can you picture Gaga working at Lidl?

If you seriously believe this sort of life is for you, there's probably a doctor somewhere who can help. But if you don't want to talk to one and really, REALLY believe you can ride the fame monster, then here are some simple steps as to how to go about it.

BE PECULIAR

Most people in the world are normal – if you want to stand out, you have to be different. But you don't want to be threatening, or seem like you should be locked up – you have to be likeable. You're going for peculiar and interesting.

Let's take Gaga as an example. She dropped out of New York University to pursue music full-time, sang and go-go danced in small clubs, and was already fairly peculiar.

One day she got a text message from a music producer she was working with referring to Queen's hit 'Radio Ga Ga', a song everyone knows – but the phone's automatic spelling software turned it into Lady Gaga. A persona was born, and before long she had reinvented herself as an avant-garde artiste replicating Andy Warhol's Factory.

Ostentatiously peculiar, see?

Along the way, she manipulated social media for all it was worth. She was the first artist to get 1 billion views on YouTube, and at the time of writing has 60.4 million Facebook fans, 75.6 million on Twitter, and even 10.1 million on Google+ which, as already explained, hardly anyone uses.

She has also found herself, in increasingly desperate

efforts to be retweetable, dressed in nothing but shells on a visit to a chip shop.

She's even launched her own social network, which you're advised not to seek out in case you end up digging your brains out with a spoon.

Stefani is now completely Gaga, in every way, and it is the all-encompassing nature of social media that makes it impossible for her to be anything else.

Even if she retired tomorrow and became a recluse, there'd always be someone tweeting that they just saw her in a shop, or commenting on her hair. She couldn't work as a piano teacher, or give all the cash away, or do anything but be Gaga for evermore.

Which is why she rings up her team every morning, demanding to be more Gaga today than yesterday, and also possibly why she's starting to wear a little thin: 2011 album *Born This Way* sold 1.1 million copies in its first week, whereas 2016's *Joanne* did a more modest 170,000.

BE HALF FAMOUS TO SOMEONE SOMEWHERE

If you're already a little bit famous – even if it is only as The Guy Who Sleeps In The Bus Stop In Staines – social media can make you more so.

Stephen Fry was simply a charming old luvvie, then he went on Twitter and suddenly he was taken seriously when calling for the world to boycott the 2014 Russian Winter Olympics over gay rights. No one did, of course, but it was reported on the BBC.

Then there's Charlie Sheen (again), who was merely

Martin Sheen's actor son with a few personal problems until 2011 when he used social media to announce to the world:

'I am on a drug. It's called Charlie Sheen. It's not available. If you try it once, you will die. Your face will melt off and your children will weep over your exploded body.'

In 2016 it was revealed that around this time Sheen had been diagnosed with HIV, which may have accounted for some of what followed.

On his drug use: 'I probably took more than anybody could survive...I was bangin' seven-gram rocks and finishing them because that's how I roll, because I have one speed, one gear...I'm different. I have a different constitution, I have a different brain, I have a different heart. I got tiger blood, man. Dying's for fools, dying's for amateurs.'

On why he likes to date porn stars: 'They're the best at what they do and I'm the best at what I do. And together it's like, it's on. Sorry, Middle America. Yeah, I said it.'

He also called himself a 'warlock' who had destroyed his 'puny maggot' of a TV producer 'with my words. Imagine what I would have done with my fire breathing fists.'

Shortly afterwards, it was reported his dad was planning an intervention. He's recently started tweeting in haikus, and his HIV is reportedly under control. As a result of all this he now has 12.3 million people paying attention to him, which goes to show a bit of fame can grow into a lot online. And don't forget that Charlie used to be a personable light comic actor.

SING AND TWEET AT THE SAME TIME

As described earlier, YouTube gave the world Justin Bieber with a few videos uploaded by his mum. His manager decided to build his social media profile before even releasing a record, and it's paid dividends with 95.3 million loyal fans hanging on his every Instagram.

It's also come close to destroying his reputation, with videos posted of him peeing in a cleaner's mop bucket while chanting 'F*** Bill Clinton' and photos going up on Instagram of a drag race on public streets in Miami, followed by his arrest, a plea deal to admit resisting an officer, and court-ordered anger management. He still has plenty of fans.

One person they went right off is James Arthur, who won *X Factor* and a £1 million record deal in 2012 and was reported to have been dropped by his label a mere 18 months later, although he denied it. It was something of a record, even for the record business.

His downfall came via Twitter, which he found himself unable to understand. He picked fights with other singers, and used it to perv over female fans and ask them round to his place, before embarrassing kiss-and-tells revealed he tended to wear his socks during the act of coitus.

Online, he called an unknown rapper 'a f***ing queer' and ranted about how much he hated his life, his fame and his record label's promotional staff.

He was forced into a humiliating apology for his behaviour, which is about as un-rock'n'roll as you can get.

When his record label took over his Twitter account, he

grabbed it back while they weren't looking to complain they were trying to persuade people to buy his album for Mother's Day.

'Stick to promoting Paul Potts please,' he sneered, referring to a previous *X Factor* contestant with a reputation for mum-friendly music, before likening himself to a captive killer whale who was being exploited.

He parted ways with his label, was humiliated, then – thanks in part to a social media following and perhaps a little maturity – re-signed with the same label a couple of years later and released a new album which went to number one.

He's even performed on *The One Show*, which is about as socially acceptable to mums as it's possible to get. If you go down this route of singing your way to social media success, remember: don't be an idiot, and take your socks OFF first.

GO VIRAL

This is not to be taken literally – catching a contagious disease is unlikely to help you achieve any of your goals.

But it might be worth taking a leaf out of the book of comedy duo Vegard and Bård Ylvisåker, who are sort of the Norwegian equivalent of Ant and Dec but taller. The brothers began making parody pop songs to air on their TV show, including one titled 'What Does The Fox Say?' It was intended as a piss-take, featuring lyrics about dogs going woof and cats going meow before the fox says, 'Ring-ding-ding-ding-dingeringeding! Gering-ding-ding-ding-dingeringeding! Gering-ding-ding-ding-dingeringeding!'

Along with a video of a singer in a man-sized fox suit, it was so bizarre that everyone who saw it had to tell someone else – and it went viral.

It had 100 million YouTube views in 35 days, shot into the music charts worldwide, and even led to a children's book which debuted at number one on *The New York Times* bestseller list.

Going viral is tricky because no one's quite sure how it works. Posting a video of you licking the dog's bum would be bizarre, but is that how you want to achieve fame? It has to be something fascinating but fun – like a sex tape, perhaps.

MAKE A SEX TAPE

This has worked for so many people it must be included, although with the broad caveat that if your sexual tastes are unusual, your appearance unattractive or your moral threshold higher than Earth's core, you will find it tricky to pull off. What you will need for this is beauty and just one goal: to be rich and famous. All other concerns will get in your way.

Paris Hilton was a scion of the hotel-owning dynasty and a socialite with nothing to do but shop and party when boyfriend Rick Salomon filmed them *in flagrante*. The tape found its way online in 2003 under the title 'One Night In Paris', and the poor girl was so upset – 'I just felt so betrayed' – that she was barely able to grasp the many offers of work which began to rain down upon her.

Within months she was signed up to a reality show whose first episode drew 13 million viewers and a year later she launched her own 'lifestyle brand', whatever that is. It seems to include selling Paris-branded hair extensions, perfume, handbags, jewellery, shoes, clothes, dog clothes, hair vitamins…

Along the way she was jailed for driving offences, started a music career, fought legal battles over her privacy and now has 44 chain stores worldwide and an estimated self-made fortune of $100 million – all from one little tape.

But while Paris has been consigned to the history section of social media, her chum Kim Kardashian got her whole family involved.

Kim was unknown until her sex tape with rapper Ray J went public, but within months her entire extended family were signed up to a reality show. These days she has her own clothing line, calendars, and a waxwork in the New York branch of Madame Tussauds, as well as equally famous sisters Kourtney, Khloe, Kylie and Kendall, mother Kris and transgender Olympian stepfather Caitlyn Jenner.

Kim, now married to uber-rapper Kanye West and a mother-of-three, is on her own worth an estimated $175 million. When she posed nude for *Paper* magazine, the pictures were so sought-after that they were released with the hashtag #Breaktheinternet. She's easily more famous than Paris.

BUT BEWARE! Ray J and Rick Salomon were never heard from again. Sex tapes can go horribly wrong and kill off whatever career you currently have if you're male.

Just ask *EastEnders* actor Leslie Grantham. The ageing star was discovered using his dressing room for online sexy-time. When the story ended up in the papers, complete with a screenshot of him sucking his finger while discussing his fantasies and opinions of fellow cast members on Skype, it was the death knell for his TV career.

He was suspended for two months, his character was killed off within a year, and when last heard of he was in low-budget movies and considering a move to Bulgaria. For why, you might ask? It was so long ago, why would anyone care?

Well, because of social media that finger-sucking image is usually around the third picture to pop up when anybody Googles his name. It's still shared as a joke on Facebook and Twitter, and his shame lives on long after it should.

DO SOMETHING REALLY STUPID

Perhaps you could frot a foam finger on live national TV like Miley Cyrus, or be a respectable public figure caught on tape smoking crack cocaine like Toronto mayor Rob Ford.

Or you could be as truly dense as PR executive Justine Sacco, who tweeted to her 500 followers as she boarded a flight to Cape Town: 'Going to Africa. Hope I don't get AIDS. Just kidding. I'm white!'

As a good communications professional, she then switched off her phone on the plane and, while in the air, the Twittersphere had a field day spreading her tweet, vilifying it, parodying it, and starting the hashtag

#HasJustineLandedYet. When she did finally turn her phone on after landing, she was horrified, apologised to all concerned, and was fired. She's since revealed how traumatising she found the public shaming, and that she can't even go on a date because every potential lover Googles her first.

Two lessons here: first, don't do something that will get you fired, and secondly don't forget there are two types of monsters. The fun type, and the type you don't want to be.

BE CUTE

Miles Scott was a five-year-old from San Francisco just getting to the end of his treatment for leukaemia. He was fascinated by superheroes and the Make-A-Wish Foundation decided to give him a treat, sending out a request for a few hundred people to help him be 'Batkid' and rescue a damsel in distress.

What Miles got was 12,000 volunteers, city officials, businesses and supporters who turned his home town into Gotham City, complete with a Batman actor and Bat-branded black Lamborghinis. He rescued a damsel tied to train tracks, stopped the Riddler raiding a bank and chased the Penguin before getting a tweet from Barack Obama. The *San Francisco Chronicle* even produced a Gotham version with the headline 'Batkid Saves City'.

People lined the streets to chant 'Batkid, Batkid', and all because of social media. Remind people of this whenever they say the Internet is evil. Miles is currently in remission.

INCLUDE CATS IF POSSIBLE

Any kind of cat will do. Kitten videos, cats playing with doorstoppers, Tumblrs of cats looking confused, blogging about life from a cat's point of view, cats playing the piano, cartoon cats, Instagramming your cat's life of disdain – it all works. Humans suck this stuff up like cat-obsessed sponges.

They don't even have to be cute. Grumpy Cat was launched onto the world with a few pictures on the sharing site Reddit, along with a gadget to help people add their own captions. The cat looked very grumpy indeed, due to a form of dwarfism, and humanity found this so hysterical that before long he had 8.7 million likes on Facebook, was on the front page of *The Wall Street Journal,* and had a business selling t-shirts, mugs, soft toys and his own line of cappuccinos. They're called Grumpuccinos.

DO NOT ATTEMPT DEAD CATS. The entire Internet will seek revenge.

GO TO SPACE

Commander Chris Hadfield had been to space three times before the world noticed him doing it. On his final mission, as commander of the International Space Station, he chronicled life 250 miles up via Twitter, Facebook and Tumblr, posting pictures of Earth below that blew our minds.

People were reminded that the ISS was up there and heard what life was like aboard, the science involved and the international cooperation. He even had Twitter chats with William Shatner, Capt. James T. Kirk himself.

Then Cdr Hadfield put a video of himself singing David Bowie's 'Space Oddity' on YouTube and the world went mental. There was the video of a man playing a guitar in space. While floating in zero gravity. While singing about space and zero gravity. It got 38.4 million views and turned a fairly plain, moustached Canadian into the top item on the evening news and an international celebrity.

So there you are – nine ways to be monstrous on social media, should you want to. But there are a million pitfalls to beware of because you're not just talking to your friends down the pub. Your social media accounts are linked to you, your computer and your address, and you have a legal responsibility for everything you do.

Which can get you in a right mess, unless you follow the rules in the next chapter.

ENGAGE BRAIN

Step 1 Open social media account.
Step 2 Congratulations, you are now a journalist.

Well, of course you're not. But as far as the law is concerned, you very much are.

Granted, you've not done much in the way of training. Some of you take a rather scattergun approach to punctuation and the average trainee on a local weekly free paper could probably write you under the table.

Never mind all that.

If you publish material online, even if it is only a description of why you had a funny dream last night or what you fancy for dinner, then you are Fleet Street now.

Let's try not to think about the fact that your average Fleet Street hack will probably have done several years of training either on the job or in a degree. Let's try to forget that they have to learn about the law, the democratic process, and shorthand.

That sort of thing relates to the days when journalists were journalists and civilians weren't.

Now we have this thing called social media, which we use, depending on skills and taste, to make friends/get laid/find information/drone on about nothing much at all. It has become a combined human consciousness, if you think humanity doesn't include people who have other things to do with their time.

As we have seen, it is also a place where news is made, spread, broken and repaired. Celebrities use it to 'get their view across' (also known as 'selling stuff'); politicians use it to 'get their view across' (also known as 'public relations'); civilians use it to peek and spy and interact; and journalists use it to do what they always have – watch, listen, report, unearth.

The problem is that this is not a psychic network where we exchange thoughts and gossip privately. It's public. It's publishing, folks – just like having your own TV channel or newspaper.

You pick who contributes, you inflate the bits you think are best, and as editor of this enterprise, you bear the ultimate responsibility for everything that passes across your screen.

So if you're to do it without getting seriously caught out, you probably want to bone up on all the laws they teach journalists from day one.

That's all the legislation relating to libel, contempt of court, sexual offences, constitutional affairs, electoral legislation, police procedural rules, lifelong anonymity orders, family courts, the Children and Young Persons Act, coroner's courts, time limitation, the Human Rights Act (fors and againsts), trespass, ownership, civil and criminal courts, indecency, subterfuge, and national security.

On day two, there's more: ethical standards, public interest (YOU try defining it to everyone's satisfaction), editorial agenda, regulatory rules and punishments, and the importance of taking a good shorthand note, which is why you will spend days three to 74 learning what is effectively a second alphabet.

Then, and only then, would you be let loose under the supervision of a hungover superior to carefully dissect an inane press release. If you manage it without incurring legal or editorial wrath, you can move on to something else.

That's how journalism works – you learn all you can, then you see what you can do without getting into trouble.

Social media is the other way around. You get into trouble, and then try to figure out why.

PEACHES

So let's consider the cautionary case of Peaches Geldof, daughter of Live Aid founder Sir Bob and his late TV presenter wife Paula Yates.

Peaches, who is sadly now also deceased at the too-young age of 25, was very proud of calling herself a journalist. It is a trade, not a profession, and as such requires no qualifications to join.

She wrote for a number of magazines and newspapers, and frequently appeared on TV. She was also often invited to 'be a celebrity' by appearing on red carpets at premieres and openings where people would ask her opinion about things, which often makes people think their opinions are right.

She wrote about fashion, and her children, and, at barely 20 at the time, could be forgiven for criticising newspapers with the comment that they write in 'pidgin English with all these terrible colloquialisms, the phrasing of which is just, like, embarrassing'.

Then she had a little rant on Twitter about 'intrusion' into the private lives of Nigella Lawson and Charles Saatchi, even though the intrusion was in the form of a court case, which are held in public because secret court cases only happen in places like Zimbabwe.

She followed this up with tweets about the trial and conviction of Lostprophets singer Ian Watkins for child sex offences. Peaches wrote: 'I can't even bring myself to comment.'

Then she commented on it at such length that she came to the attention of the police.

Peaches had criticised newspapers and other media organisations for not naming the two women convicted alongside Watkins and who had offered up their children for him to abuse.

She found the names of these women on American websites, and repeated them for her 166,366 followers laced with a heavy dollop of eau de Watergate, like any other journalist exposing the truth the mainstream media were conspiring to keep quiet.

Sadly for Peaches, sadly for those who retweeted her, and for those who shared the names on British websites and who by so doing had republished Peaches' original publication – this was the wrong thing to do.

Britain has a strict law guaranteeing anonymity for victims of sexual offences. In this case, the children who were abused.

Naming their mothers would identify them, as any trainee hack with four seconds' experience could have told her.

As it was, South Wales Police had to investigate complaints about Peaches' tweets and the Attorney General was prompted into issuing a public telling-off.

It is quite unreasonable for the law to expect everyone with access to a computer to have the same working knowledge of legislation as a qualified journalist.

LAW'S MERCILESS REACH

But the law does expect it. And it is merciless in enforcing it.

The Speaker's wife, Sally Bercow, and comedian Alan Davies were both ordered to pay £15,000 for tweets judged to have wrongly identified the late Lord McAlpine as the target of a paedophilia allegation. Unfortunately for them, he wasn't late at the time. Or, indeed, a paedophile.

Friends and family of footballer Ched Evans, who was convicted and at a retrial acquitted of rape, were fined for naming his accuser on social media because they believed she had lied.

Jon Venables, who as a ten-year-old took part in the murder of toddler James Bulger, has been frequently pictured and identified online despite a lifelong court order protecting his anonymity to prevent vigilante attacks. There have been a series of court punishments for those who have broken the order.

Everyone knows, in the calmness of their common sense, that you don't name rape victims, don't accuse millionaires of child abuse without proof, and don't break court orders.

But social media is rarely calm, and people often forget.

TEACH YOURSELF MEDIA LAW

You can shortcut all that legal training with a few short points to help you navigate your way around the legal pitfalls online:

- If you write anything online, you are a legally recognised publisher. Put it on a business card or something – make the most of it.

- Resharing someone else's false allegation gets you in less trouble than if you type it afresh yourself. But if you reshare something you think might get you in trouble, you probably shouldn't be doing it.

- Remember – if a newspaper hasn't named someone (because they really like naming people) there's probably a damned good reason.

Those are just tips for avoiding trouble with the authorities. What about if you get in trouble with a person?

Few people realise that if you enter into a sexual relationship with someone, you have a duty of confidentiality to that person in law. It's almost never enforced, but it's worth bearing in mind if a) you decide to publish intimate pictures of a cheating ex on Facebook; and b) your ex knows the law, or has enough money to pay someone else to know the law for them.

And remember the case of mum Sharon Smith, 47, from Bexleyheath, who was left with a £20,000 bill over comments she wrote on her private, hard-to-see Facebook page.

Her remarks about a certain school governor were picked up by one of the few people with access and reposted onto a public page. Lawyers were swiftly instructed and it led to a libel case in the High Court.

A family member, friend or lover could sue you for invading their privacy. If you Instagram a picture taken in private circumstances, post their bank account number and bank balance on a blog, or perhaps share a picture of their children without permission, you can get in big trouble very quickly.

Of course, if you're on friendly terms, it can be quickly resolved by an apology and deletion of the offending material – but if you breach the privacy of someone on the other side of a family vendetta, a custody battle, or who was in their garden minding their own business, then you're on a sticky wicket.

RESPECTING PRIVACY

So be aware that in the UK, privacy law comes down to just 17 words in Article 8 of the Human Rights Act 1998 – stating that every individual has a right to respect for their privacy.

If you think you can show that whatever you did respected their privacy, then you will probably be fine.

So, when using social media to publish the fallout of your bitter break-up:

- Photoshop out the bank account number on the top of his statement showing how many times he took that trollop to your favourite restaurant.

- Post a happy family picture with a caption about how your cheating wife has walked out on your two sobbing children, by all means, but blur the children's faces first.

- Tweet as often as you like about your appalling neighbour and their naff Leylandii hedge which is ruining your life, but make sure YOU'RE not identifiable from the account and nor are they.

- If you must blog about the strange sexual peccadilloes of that person you met at the tennis club, change the names, places and dates. Or get them to sign a release.

But wait, that's not all – even if you've managed to avoid upsetting people, you can always get into legal trouble with the police, businesses and corporations.

If they're your employer, remember they could fire you for something you write online. PC Tony Ryan was dismissed for gross misconduct after 800 tweets were sent from an account that referred to professional standards officers as 'scum' and 'lower than slime'. PC Ryan denied the Twitter account involved was his, but Avon and Somerset Police thought they knew better.

BIG BUSINESS

Businesses almost always have lawyers, but the people who run them are usually too busy to be searching for any and all references to themselves on the Internet.

Some firms do – utility companies like BT and Thames Water are big enough (and bad enough) to employ social media teams who cruise these sites looking for complaints, and then dedicate themselves to sorting out whatever the problem may be.

This is a positive, and very productive, way of using social media both to complain and to improve your customer service. It is also worth bearing in mind when your electricity bill soars unexpectedly – try tweeting the company responsible in the hope that they are shamed into reducing it.

But very occasionally, companies handle social media reputation issues the wrong way.

Controversial payday loan company Wonga got on its high horse when it realised that a Twitter account with a mere 1,200 followers had tweeted a picture doctored to include a character from one of its adverts. Unfortunately for the tweeter concerned, the picture into which he had inserted elderly Earl from the Wonga adverts was a section of a Hogarth painting about the life of the poor. Worse still, he'd photoshopped on the caption: 'Fed up of final demands, whining relatives and Debtors' Prison? Wonga.com. Your soul is ours.'

Now, satire is allowed in English law – just about. But Wonga fired off a lawyer's letter to Twitter and the user, claiming they had breached copyright law by using a copyrighted image in the form of a character from their adverts.

They could even have claimed the satire was defamatory – that Wonga was purchasing souls – except a judge would most likely say it was clearly a joke.

At the time of writing, the satirical image can still be found on Twitter, as Wonga's legal letter had done nothing but highlight it to thousands of people who hadn't noticed it previously, and reshared it out of pure devilment.

THE STREISAND EFFECT

This is known in the world of social media as 'The Streisand Effect'. It came into being after American entertainer Barbra Streisand launched a $50 million lawsuit against a photographer and a website for invading her privacy by publishing a picture of her oceanfront house.

Unfortunately for Babs, the picture titled 'Image 3850' was in a set of 12,000 California coastline photos all of which were publicly available online.

Before she filed a lawsuit, her house had been looked at just six times, two of which were by her own lawyers; a month after the suit was filed and the story covered by the media, it had been viewed 420,000 times.

Sometimes, making a fuss about something you don't like just means more people know about it. If social media has a characteristic, it is mischievousness. If it looks fun, or interesting, or just plain daft, the Internet will be all over it like a rash.

DON'T USE THE 'B' WORD

On the topic of daft, there is no better example than the Twitter Joke Trial.

Perhaps you've heard of it, because it did make the telly news, but then again perhaps not. Every bluffer needs to know that it affects every single person on social media, and in fact every person in the country who thinks they know what a joke is.

In 2010, trainee accountant Paul Chambers was catching a flight from Robin Hood Airport in Yorkshire in order to visit his girlfriend. Due to bad weather, the airport was closed and his flight cancelled.

In response to this spanner in his romantic plans, Paul opened his Twitter and typed: 'Crap! Robin Hood airport is closed. You've got a week and a bit to get your shit together otherwise I'm blowing the airport sky high!!'

He sent the tweet, which was seen by whichever of his 600 or so followers were online at the time. And then he went home to rearrange his travel plans.

Nothing else happened. No bombs, no explosions, no genuine or real fears that a trainee accountant was going to blow up an airport.

A week later while doing an unrelated Internet search, an off-duty manager saw the tweet and dutifully reported it to management, who decided quite sensibly that it was not a threat.

But they also thought they ought to tell the police, just in case, and Paul was arrested at his office. His house was searched, and his mobile phone, laptop and computer were confiscated.

He was charged with 'sending a public electronic message that was grossly offensive or of an indecent, obscene or menacing character contrary to the Communications Act 2003'. A few months later, he was found guilty by magistrates, fined £385 and told to pay £600 costs.

So far so foolish. A bit heavy-handed of PC Plod of course, but we can't have people going around making silly jokes about bombs.

Convictions are frowned upon in the accountancy world, and Paul lost not only that job but all prospects of getting another one. His career went down the pan and so, in the spirit of pointing out that the law was being an ass and not doing what it was designed for, he appealed against the conviction.

By this time, a few other tweeters had heard about it. Stephen Fry offered to pay his legal costs and tweeting lawyer David Allen Green took on the case.

But when the appeal judge ruled the tweet was 'menacing' and said the conviction must stand, the issue went global.

I AM SPARTACUS

Tens of thousands of people republished Paul's original tweet under their own accounts, adding the hashtag #iamspartacus in a reference to the Kirk Douglas movie in which Spartacus's fellow slaves protected him from the Romans who were hunting him.

Suddenly, the question of what jokes the law would allow – under any circumstances, not just social media – focused everyone's mind.

A High Court appeal could not reach a conclusion, and it was not until a third appeal in 2012 that three judges finally decided that, yes, Paul had made a terrible joke, but it was about as menacing as a meringue.

The whole affair cost a fortune, took more than two years, and put a young man under incredible pressure when he'd merely wanted to joke to friends about how hacked off he was about the airport being shut.

But he did finally walk out of the High Court with his conviction quashed, his accountancy career once more viable, and as a minor media star and hero of Twitter.

More importantly, he set a legal precedent that something which is quite obviously a joke and not meant to be taken seriously should not get you arrested, fired, convicted or otherwise in serious trouble.

The Lord Chief Justice said: 'Satirical or iconoclastic or rude comment, the expression of unpopular or unfashionable opinion about serious or trivial matters, banter or humour, even if distasteful to some or painful to those subjected to it should and no doubt will continue at their customary level, quite undiminished.'

Jokes are allowed – but it would be wise for the best bluffers to remember that the law can and will always get things wrong.

THE BASIC RULES

All of this boils down to three basic things – defamation, privacy and humour. You don't want to get on the wrong side of any of them.

And naturally, there are three basic rules for steering clear of trouble.

You might be the only person who thinks it's funny. If you think this is likely, don't put it online. If you're not arrested, you will almost certainly have to deal with lots of people telling you that you're a twat.

1. If you can't prove it, don't write it.
2. If you can't justify publishing something no one else knows, don't do it.
3. Remember, you never know who's watching.

Failing that, it might be an idea to become a lawyer. They're the only ones who seem to survive a legal minefield with their skins intact.

They've no sense of humour, though.

SOCIAL MEDIA? LOL

Luckily for us all, the Internet is not filled with lawyers. They're just there trying to keep a check on things, and often make a total hash of it because they have no idea what 'funny' is.

Rather, the Internet is filled with cats. And people pretending to be their cat. And techno-geeks thinking of new ways to make videos of cats who look like they're dancing, Hitler, or just grumpy.

WHAT'S SO FUNNY?

The good bluffer knows that there are three basic types of people online, and the rules for dealing with them:

1. People who want to sue someone
This is the simplest of the three categories, and covers lawyers, litigious types, thin-skinned billionaires and vengeful sorts.

RULE Do not engage with these people.

It's rarely worth it. Lawyers don't hand out free legal advice, litigious types sue at the drop of a hat, thin-skinned billionaires don't even wait for the hat to drop and vengeful types are simply insane. You'd avoid them in real life – avoid them on social media, wherever possible. The likelihood of getting into serious trouble if you do not is very high.

The only exception to this rule is if you 'do a Spartacus' and need a social media-savvy lawyer/handy celebrity to argue your case.

2. People who want to be entertained

This is the second easiest category of people to keep happy online.

RULE Be entertaining.

You don't have to pirouette naked on roller skates in a viral YouTube video, but they won't mind if you do. Half of them will clap wildly, 40 per cent will think a cat would be funnier, and 10 per cent will bother to write a comment criticising your technique. It doesn't matter; whether they loved it or hated it, they were entertained for a few brief moments.

Perhaps roller-skating's not your thing. Fine, so be entertaining in terms of the information you impart, the pictures you can take, and the music you share. The boredom thresholds of people in this category are so low they're close to Earth's core, so even if you're not a natural entertainer, they won't be paying attention to you for long. A quick bit of TA DA! and they'll leave you alone.

3. People who think they're funny

This is the trickiest category. Most are woefully lacking in the main ingredients, and one or two really are frustrated stand-up comedians who just missed their lucky break. It's tricky in exactly the same way it's tricky to deal with these people in real life, in that natural-born comedians are by nature vain, egotistical, selfish manic depressives with a self-abuse complex.

RULE Tread carefully, for you tread on their dreams.

When a bluffer meets someone online who thinks they're funny, there are several options available:

- a) **Laugh.** Really only do this if they're genuinely funny, or you'll never be shot of them. In fact, even if they're genuinely funny, they'll love you forever if you laugh at their jokes, so you'll never be shot of them anyway. But still, if it's a good joke, let them know.

- b) **Ignore them.** This is frankly the best way of dealing with someone who thinks they're funny but isn't. The bonus of doing it online is they don't know you heard what they said, tutted and picked your nose; they think if anyone didn't laugh it's a technical glitch. If you ignore them long enough, they might think your computer is broken and go off and bother someone else.

- c) **Point out why they're not funny.** This is for only a confident bluffer, because it can go seriously wrong. Dissecting a joke is the most humourless thing you can do, so there is a strong chance of Internet opprobrium rebounding onto you. If you plump for option c), you have to be able to bluff the non-amusing person that you're still on their side. So remember the ingredients for humour are wit, timing and audience, and explain where they're missing one or all three.

For example: 'That's really funny, it's just a shame you only have four followers. What's wrong with people?'

Or: 'I don't object to humorous remarks about famous people you'd like to shag, but it's probably best not to mention the one whose name is currently trending worldwide, because he's been found dead in a pool of his own vomit. Also, you ought to take him off your list.'

Or: 'That would be EVEN funnier if only you could spell fellatio.'

The bluffer needs to know there are many ways to be funny on social media other than just telling jokes. If you find yourself stuck for a funny gag, perhaps you can use one of these to make yourself sound amusing or knowledgeable.

CRAZES

If there's one thing for which social media can be relied upon, it's taking one little thing and making it a phenomenon, a happening that spreads around the world and that everyone with a social media account wants to be part of.

However, as it's humans doing the crazing, there are good crazes and bad crazes.

Every bluffer should know the best example of a good craze is the Ice Bucket Challenge, in which people videoed themselves having a bucket of iced water poured over their heads and then nominating others to do the same, in order to raise awareness and funds for a number of serious illnesses including ALS, which Professor Stephen Hawking has had for 52 years, also known as motor neurone disease.

It went viral – i.e., infected social media like a dose of the bubonic plague – in the summer of 2014. The origins are unclear, but it may have begun with Pete Frates, a Boston college student who was diagnosed with ALS in 2012. Being covered in cold water while videoed was also used around the same time to raise money for cancer research, children with brain tumours, and pet charities.

It coalesced into the Ice Bucket Challenge, the rules of which involved being soaked, nominating others to do the same, and if they did not within 24 hours they had to donate to charity.

These rules of course meant that by getting soaked you didn't have to donate, and virtually everyone who took part ignored them.

YouTube cites 4.4 million videos tagged 'Ice Bucket Challenge', while on Facebook there were another 2.4 million – and 28 million likes, comments or posts. Instagram had a further 3.7 million videos.

Celebrities who soaked themselves – and massively increased the spread of the craze – included the Beckhams, Justin Timberlake, Taylor Swift, Whoopi

Goldberg, Dolly Parton (in her wig), Bill Gates, Lady Gaga (dressed as a dominatrix) and Justin Bieber, who was criticised for not having any ice in his bucket.

Barack Obama refused, but donated anyway.

In the USA, the main ALS charity raised almost $100 million in the same period it would normally raise $2.7 million. In the UK, the MND Association got £2.7 million in a week when it would normally get about £200,000.

It raised lots of money, so it was good. But the BBC has reported only one in ten people who took part actually donated, so it could have been better.

There are plenty of bad crazes out there too, often associated with teenagers. In early 2015 there were fears about the Charlie Charlie Challenge, in which teens try to communicate with a Mexican ghost called Charlie Charlie.

Using the well-known supernatural device of two pencils arranged in a cross, they then ask him for advice about dating, homework and when Justin Bieber will release his next album. The craze led to reports that impressionable youngsters around the world had become convinced that Charlie had entered their smart devices with ghostly messages.

But far more serious was a social media craze called Neknominate, which began in Australia in 2014 with young people nominating one another to down a pint of beer in one gulp and upload video evidence of this feat. The successful drinker then nominates two others to do the same within 24 hours.

A beer every 24 hours isn't too bad, right? Only those taking part got more ambitious, nominating more potent drinks and more extreme activities to be undertaken while imbibing them.

In July 2015 Callum Clatworthy-Robins, 22, of Wales, admitted causing unnecessary suffering to a goldfish after being filmed swallowing one live during a game of Neknominate. A year earlier, Terry Gallop, 29, of Salisbury, Wiltshire, swallowed a cocktail of goldfish, ketchup, vinegar, Jack Daniels, mint, soy sauce and lager on his birthday and was later fined £818 after admitting an offence under the Animal Welfare Act.

Perhaps unsurprisingly, Neknominate has been accused of causing the deaths of five people in the UK, including rugby fan Stephen Brookes, 29, of Cardiff, who died after being filmed drinking three quarters of a bottle of vodka. In Ireland, 19-year-old Jonny Byrne died after jumping into a river as part of his nomination, leading his family to call for an end to the craze.

MEMES

A meme is, at its root, an idea which spreads from person to person like a virus. A bluffer given to grandiosity might say that the very first memes were religions – or making fire, or banging two stones together.

Online, a meme is A Funny Thing that everybody found So Funny that they did the Same Funny Thing themselves until eventually Everyone Was Doing It and it Stopped Being Funny. The best ones start by accident, and the worst ones are those that some polo-necked hipster came up with in a marketing meeting for a corporation's brand reinvention.

Recently, the Department for Culture, Media and Sport suggested people 'make your own meme!' to celebrate Shakespeare's birthday by adding a quote to a picture of a man with a donkey's head. It didn't storm the Internet; perhaps they should have used a cat.

Internet memes basically boil down to taking a well-known quote or image from a movie, and twisting it to suit any and every situation.

The Wonka meme is a classic of the genre – taking Gene Wilder's bitchy chocolate entrepreneur and using it to be condescending and sarcastic about everything. There's 'Oh, so you drink Starbucks? How intellectually enlightened you must be,' 'Oh, so you're witty on the Internet? I bet that translates well into the real world,' and 'Oh, you make memes in your spare time? You must feel so accomplished.'

Every bluffer needs to know the Wonka meme is so dead it can only be found on the third page of Google. Or in a museum.

When Boromir's 'One does not simply walk into Mordor' quote from *The Lord of the Rings* became a meme, it started off geeky and just got geekier. First Boromir was replaced by Data from *Star Trek: The Next Generation,* saying, 'One does not simply…warp into Mordor.' Then he was replaced by the General Lee from the 1980s TV show *Dukes of Hazzard* and the phrase: 'One does not simply…take the short cut over the Old Mill Road to Mordor, YEEEHAAAWWW!' Which goes to show, someone can always outgeek you.

A really good bluffer, when they see a meme developing, does not take part in it. They set up a website where people can add their own captions to pictures, generating their own memes, and rake in the advertising cash.

Other classic memes include Rickrolling, a way of tricking someone – anyone, really – into clicking a link under the impression it will lead to something interesting, but in fact leads only to a video of Rick Astley singing his 1987 hit 'Never Gonna Give You Up'. A cynic would suggest the whole thing was started by Rick's agent after he realised his client would never have a more culturally relevant song; good bluffers will know that in 2010 it was reported that Rick got a mere $12 in performance royalties from YouTube, because he didn't write the track. A really excellent bluffer can add that the video has been deleted and reposted several times and so far 136 million people are thought to have been Rickrolled since it started in 2007.

There are too many memes to list them all, but the one every bluffer needs to know is LOLcats because this is how felines came to bestride the Internet as though they were some kind of spitting, clawing, predatory beast you wouldn't leave alone with children.

By the mid-00s, digital cameras were everywhere and people were using this amazing technological development to shoot home-made porn and take pictures of their…pets. LOLcats.com was set up in 2006 and is simply a collection of funny cat pictures to which owners could add their own captions, usually in the style of a cat's inner monologue and invariably using a shouty font. Cue pictures of cats that were cute, bizarre, funny, or pulling faces.

It was soon followed by I Can Has Cheezburger?, which was much the same thing and got 1.5 million hits a day at its peak. The captions are generally misspelt and grammar-free, written in the style of felines whose owners believe that, if they could talk, it would be like babies with lots of pointy teeth.

A good bluffer will say 'LOLcats really made the Impact font the only one suitable for Internet humour.' A fantastic bluffer will point out LOLcats actually began in the 1870s, when British photographer Harry Pointer put cats in fancy dress for Victorian picture postcards.

PARODIES

This is when people take something terribly famous, and take the piss.

So some bright spark decided the President of the USA's website www.whitehouse.gov was lacking in a sense of humour, and set up www.whitehouse.net which offers second-hand spy planes for sale and runs spoof news about the White House being painted green. Then there's Wickerpedia, an online encyclopaedia of everything you might want to know about hand-woven plant fibres.

(The main thing you need to know about funny stuff on the Internet is that it's all done by people with too much time on their hands.)

One of the more irritating – and financially successful, for someone – is the 'Keep Calm And Carry On' motivational poster produced by the British Government in 1939. Few people noticed it at the time, preoccupied as they were by the prospect of a Nazi invasion.

In 2000 bookstore owner Stuart Manley came across an original poster tucked in with a box of old books, and was so taken with it that he framed it and put it up behind the till of his shop in Alnwick, Northumberland. Customers liked it so much he started selling copies, and lo, an Internet phenomenon was born.

Stuart's wife Mary said: 'I didn't want it trivialised. But now of course it's been trivialised beyond belief.'

And how. Various firms have tried to register the slogan as a trademark, and it's since been used to decorate mugs, t-shirts, and even shanghaied into selling McFly tickets when they called their 2012 tour 'Keep Calm And Play Louder'.

It is now possible to buy, in just about any format from key rings to duvet covers, 'Keep Calm And Say You'll Marry Me', 'Stay Alive And Avoid Zombies', 'Now Panic And Freak Out' and 'Don't Panic And Fake A British Accent'.

Online, there are any number of Keep Calm poster generators where you can make your own version of the original, complete with the right font and crown.

If only Hitler knew what he'd done.

Possibly the best parodies to be found are the ones which take a crucial scene from 2004 German war movie *Downfall* and turn it into social commentary on, well, just about anything.

In the original, Hitler receives bad news from his generals during the last days in his Berlin bunker, and sends half of them out of the room before having a screaming meltdown at the remaining few.

The parodies retain the imagery and German dialogue,

but use subtitles to depict Hitler having a meltdown about, variously:

- Twitter crashing again ('Don't they care about their users? Don't they care about us Tweeple?')

- Finding out Sheffield United has been relegated ('And to make matters worse, it's Unsworth who scores. IT'S UNSWORTH WHO SCORES.')

- Grammar Nazis ('You guys are like some kind of grammar authorities or some, some kind of grammar… strict police…dammit! What's the word I'm looking for? I'm thinking of an authoritarian regime or something with the streets filled with, like, uniformed soldiers that arrest people for the slightest offence. It was on the tip of my tongue, goddamn it. Well, you know what I mean.')

And the best of the best, as any bluffer knows, is the one where Hitler finds out about all the Hitler *Downfall* parodies and screams: 'I slaughtered millions, cut a bloody path of destruction across Europe, and for what? So I could be the latest juvenile web fad, no better than YouTube Fred or that stupid f-----g hamster?'

BLUFFER'S TIP *Don't ever let anyone tell you the greatest Internet parody was Star Wars Kid.*

This was a video of 15-year-old Ghyslain Raza from Quebec, who filmed himself fighting an imaginary foe with a golf ball retriever as a double-ended lightsaber. In each successive take, he gets more into the role of a Sith lord, and starts making sound effect noises. He was a chubby kid too, so it looked extra awkward.

Ghyslain made the video privately for a school project but left it lying around. Other students found it and posted it online in 2003, when videos and memes were so rare that they hung about for years.

It's been seen by around a billion people in different formats, with 33.8 million views on YouTube alone and 58,000 user comments. It was parodied on TV shows *The Simpsons, South Park* and *Family Guy.* Around 140,000 signed a petition demanding Raza be given a role in the next *Star Wars* movie.

But Raza didn't enjoy it. He was arguably one of the first victims of cyberbullying, picked on at school and on the Internet where people called him 'a pox on humanity'. He said: 'What I saw was mean. It was violent. People were telling me to commit suicide...In the common room, students climbed onto tabletops to insult me. I couldn't help but feel worthless, like my life wasn't worth living.'

Raza was diagnosed with depression, dropped out of school, and spent a year in a children's psychiatric ward. He went on to graduate as a law student, and issued a $250,000 lawsuit against those who had first posted the video online without his permission, which he settled out of court. He now speaks out against cyber bullying.

RULE Don't parody someone who's not playing the game. Because that's just mean.

FAKE ACCOUNTS

As has already been stated, half the Internet is filled with people masquerading under a fake identity. The other half is people pretending they're interesting.

So there are people who tweet as the Voice of God. There are whole Tumblrs devoted to the latest OH SO CUTE pictures of people's pet cats and dogs. There are, for obvious reasons, fake dating profiles that those responsible then back up with fake social media pages.

Some people do it just for pleasure, others because they have a serious psychological condition, and one or two for darker purposes.

For example, Facebook recently admitted anything up to 270 million of its accounts (out of a total 2.1 billion) were fake or duplicates. Most were because someone had more than one account (for example if they forgot their old password, or didn't close one account before opening a new one), quite a few were misclassified (i.e., for a pet or a business), and anything up to 3 per cent or 63 million were 'undesirable' – accounts that break the rules, perhaps involving porn or spam.

They are easily spotted – bad fake accounts have limited followers and write drivel, and the good ones are funny.

Do say 'Did you know there are TEN people pretending to be Ed Balls on Twitter?'

Don't say 'OMG did you know God is on Instagram?'

WRY OBSERVATIONS

Kind of a warped version of the fake account, because this often comes down to someone pretending to be something they're not. Can be found on Tumblr, Twitter, Facebook and any other kind of social media.

So there's Things Overheard In Waitrose ('Put the Latin textbook away and help me find the quinoa, Algernon'), Texts From Mum ('DINNER IS AT FIVE BUT THAT DOESNT MEAN YOU HAVE TO WAIT UNTIL FIVE TO COME OVER WE WILL LET YOU IN EARLIER') and Damnyouautocorrect.com ('I'm drying my goat as we speak').

Do say '"Texts From Dog" actually became two books, you know. New and old media in perfect synchronicity.'

Don't say 'I've got too much work to do to spend time looking at rubbish like that.'

'The mob has many heads but no brains.'
Tim Berners-Lee, inventor of the World Wide Web

HANG 'EM HIGH

Centuries ago, mobs were formed on those occasions when several people in the village agreed someone else had been bad. They would mutter amongst themselves, grab a pitchfork, and sweep others along as they went off to storm the castle, torch the hayrick or drown the local witch.

Thanks to social media, that is now a distant memory.

These days, lynch mobs are quicker, nastier and harder for the sheriff to track down afterwards. Without physically being next to the person waving a pitchfork, our human brains see no reason not to say, 'Yeah, quite right, STONE HIM.'

Where in real life we might think, 'Oh, now, it can't be that bad, let's be sensible,' online we don't have the same fear of physical harm to make us question our actions. As a result, mobs flare up within seconds and can rampage for days.

Do say 'If Twitter was real life, we'd all have been strung up by now.'

Don't say 'Who's asking, punk?'

There are rules for how to survive these things. And the first thing you should know is how to spot a lynch mob.

Naturally, the best time to spot one is as it forms, so that you have plenty of opportunity to run away. Spotting a lynch mob after it's taken a dislike to you is a little late, and leaves you with very few options. To spot them good and early, you need to know the Life Cycle Of A Lynch Mob:

1. Someone says something bad.

2. Someone else notices.

3. The second person broadcasts the offence.

4. Each of the people who hear the news spreads it again, allowing the original offence to multiply like bacteria on a body dumped in a cesspit. The lynch mob is named Something Must Be Done, and attracts people who are more offensive than the first offender.

5. The original offence is magnified by a factor of 50 GAZILLION and the lynch mob achieves critical mass.

6. The originator of the bad thing says sorry.

7. Half of the offended people say, 'Well, don't do it again.' The other half scream, 'IT'S TOO LATE NOW!'

8. The originator of the bad thing deletes account, falls on sword, makes charitable donation, or commits suicide.

9. Most people grumble but decide enough's enough.

10. 84 people are still offended and will be forever.

There are many ways to extend this life cycle. The originator of the offence could take a ludicrously long time to apologise, either through being dense or, like Justine Sacco previously mentioned, by boarding a plane and being utterly unaware of the storm they have unleashed.

You could be offensive AND idiotic, or offensive, idiotic, AND famous, like footballer Joey Barton, who tweeted that people on benefits should have to get a licence to breed.

The apology could be lacking in sincerity. Or it could be that the original offence is so deeply appalling that people are still appalled even if it turns out it wasn't true.

THE PHONE-HACKING FURORE

Such was the case in July 2011 when *The Guardian* reported shocking news that *News of the World* journalists had hacked and then deleted the voicemails of missing schoolgirl Milly Dowler. Milly was later found dead, but at the time there was still hope she was alive.

The Guardian reported that this gave false hope to Milly's family because it gave them the impression that Milly had listened to, and deleted, her own messages. Her parents, Bob and Sally, later recounted those harrowing moments to a public inquiry.

Everyone was horrified. Online, there was widespread screaming for the *News of the World* to be boycotted, for major firms to pull advertising, and for those responsible to have their heads stuck on spikes on Tower Bridge.

The social media furore – in particular, the way so many people called, tweeted, Facebooked and demanded big companies to pull their adverts from the paper – had an impact on the parent company's share price worldwide with big falls reported in Sydney, New York and London. The *News of the World* ceased publishing just five days after *The Guardian*'s story.

It later transpired that most of the 268 journalists who lost their jobs that day had worked there for two years or less, and had nothing to do with hacking Milly's phone. This did little to stop the mob's hatred of them, and many were sent death threats on social media.

And in December of that year – five months later – *The Guardian* reported they'd got it wrong. The messages had been deleted, but it was probably done automatically by the mobile network, and possibly even as a result of the police listening to the messages.

No one gave a toss. That's what happens after a lynch mob – those who took part walk away, whistling, and don't bother to clean up the mess they leave behind. All people remember is they were JUST APPALLED about THAT THING the details of which they CAN'T QUITE REMEMBER.

The power of that lynch mob was so strong it sparked similar investigations into other newspapers, as well as separate police inquiries into corruption of public officials and computer hacking. Dozens of journalists were arrested, some convicted, and most cleared.

Do say 'Truth is the first casualty of a social media lynch mob.'

Don't say 'I can't believe you said that! I'm starting a hashtag.'

BREAKING GOOD

But all is not lost. Lynch mobs may be vicious and unthinking examples of humanity at its worst, but as with so many bad things they start out with good intentions – the wish to make bad things better. And sometimes it works.

When social media spotted an app allowing users to carry out virtual plastic surgery – sucking out fat, stitching up wounds and making an overweight woman look like Barbie – it was bad enough. But then it turned out iTunes had rated the game suitable for nine-year-olds. It caused such a fuss online that the app was pulled – hurrah!

In April 2013 the *Mail on Sunday* reported how easy it was to get help from a food bank, by lying about how destitute or hungry you were.

The article was shared 6,000 times on social media in the first day, and sparked fury that anyone was attacking a charity that helps to feed the hungry. The upshot was the charity involved had a 1,000 per cent increase in donations, amounting to £50,000, in just a few days.

WHO'S WHO IN A LYNCH MOB

There are some characters that appear in every lynch mob.

The instigator
The person who felt the offence first, and therefore is the person ostensibly in control of the lynch mob. The rest of the mob can be called off by this person, if done early enough. For example, when Olympic diver Tom Daley was sent a tweet criticising him for not winning a gold medal and saying he'd let down his (recently deceased) dad, he retweeted it to his followers who then piled in on the stupid adolescent who'd sent it.

Reece Messer, 17, bit back in further offensive tweets and by the wee hours of the morning, local police were knocking on his door. He got a formal warning for harassment and days of newspaper coverage revealing his dysfunctional upbringing, medication and life on benefits. All a bit heavy, really, and Messer blamed the overreaction on the fact that Tom did not publicly accept his apology and let the mob go after him. Perhaps true – but after the mob reaches critical mass, even the instigator can't call it back.

The celebrity
There is usually one, who's found out about what people are talking about and is either sharing the rage or trying to win popularity. Often they just share something without computing that they have 14 trillion followers who will go bonkers about it, and start lynch mobs by accident. Think of them as blundering giants and avoid.

The bandwagoner
If there's one passing, they'll jump on it. They've been offended this week already by the latest UKIP advert, Weetabix packaging, and the decision to add folic acid to flour. Happy to join any cause without necessarily knowing anything about it. Useful if you want to start a mob, and can be made to go away by giving them a different bandwagon to jump on.

The accidental fascist
Possibly the most deadly member of any lynch mob. Probably vegan, definitely a Labour supporter, quite likely a postgraduate student or member of a collective. Really, REALLY believes in Doing Things That Are Good and Hating Things That Are Bad, which is why these people will howl for the blood of anyone who eats meat, votes differently, or has an opinion they disagree with. Will happily burn books without realising this makes them A Bad Person, because as far as this person is concerned, they are always right and anyone who disagrees should be harangued, tweetstormed, or harassed to the point of suicide. Keep a bargepole between you and them at all times.

The actual fascist
Someone who genuinely believes in things that are deeply horrible to most people, and sees lynch mobs as a vehicle for expressing those views to others. For example, entering a row about abortion by telling rape victims they're selfish, or landing on the #yayforequalmarriage hashtag and telling everyone involved they're going to

burn in hell. Noticing these types is the same as giving them oxygen – you'll regret it.

Trolls
Them again. There is further examination of this gutter-dwelling subspecies in the next chapter, but for ease of spotting, these are the people who want you to die, laugh at others' misery, and have no idea how to interact with other human beings in anything approaching a normal manner. In the case of Justine Sacco, who tweeted something stupid and unfortunate about AIDS, they are the people who spent hours tweeting her telling her she was going to get raped by an AIDS sufferer. Not nice, and usually bad spellers.

Well-meaning ordinary people who are just upset
They get swept in, have no axe to grind, and will probably calm down if you say sorry and give it 24 hours.

ESCAPING THE LYNCH MOB

So you've spotted a lynch mob, you know how the lynch mob works, and you can identify who's in the lynch mob. The next step is to escape.

There are three methods of achieving this:

1. Outrun the lynch mob
This requires proper knowledge of the lynch mob life cycle and a surgical ability to intervene and terminate. If you have provoked the lynch mob, you need to apologise IMMEDIATELY and with DEEP SINCERITY.

Don't forget to promptly delete whatever caused offence; if you don't, latecomers will be offended for hours or days and the lynch mob will keep struggling back to life.

You really need to do this before the mob achieves critical mass, after which it's virtually impossible to stop. If at all possible, make sure the first person to be offended and any celebrities are apologised to first – they have the most influence in stopping the rest of the mob.

There is no point in apologising to fascists or trolls.

2. Outwit the lynch mob

When the mob cannot be stopped by an apology and deletion, you can try persuading them you've been misunderstood – that you were, rather than being offensive, being post-ironic about a thing that was offensive to you too.

If you do this early enough it might just work, but be aware that there are some instances where irony is not a reasonable excuse – joking about child abuse or the recently dead, for example.

You could also try changing the name of your social media profile, just in case it stops extra people hunting your page down to tell you how much they dislike you. Probably won't work and you'll look guilty, so only do this as a last resort.

3. Join the lynch mob

Another last resort if a mob is out to get you is to take up a pitchfork, wave it above your head, and vow revenge on the originator of the offence – EVEN IF THIS WAS YOU.

This could be a great big meta-apology, in which you harshly criticise yourself and abuse your own crass stupidity for all the world to see, which would in all likelihood confuse the rest of the mob, make them think you were mentally unwell and therefore leave you alone. *In extremis*, offer to fall on your fork.

Or joining the mob could constitute an elaborate bluff in which you express outrage at the outrageous thing, then act surprised and devastated when it turns out your account was used for this outrage, then insist that you must have been hacked because you would never say such a thing.

There are some people that would never be convinced by this, but it's worth a shot.

Finally, you can join the lynch mob by claiming you were only repeating what Someone Over There said, and so misdirect the mob to attack them. When they find no evidence of any outrageous tweet or post, say cynically, 'Well of COURSE they've deleted it,' and keep everything crossed that your innocent victim is not as sly as you.

THE NET RESULT OF ALL LYNCH MOBS

Mobs generate fear and, even if only briefly, mass conformity. Remember that people like to feel they're not alone, and by being part of a mob, they validate their opinions and belief that they are In The Right and people they don't agree with are In The Wrong. Anyone who's ever seen a good lynch mob on the rampage is rightly wary of provoking one, and in the end everyone is a little more scared of saying something unacceptable to the masses.

This is both political correctness gone mad, and normal human behaviour. Criminal and civil courts have long ruled that the human habit of gossip is the method by which civilisation regulates itself – that social disapproval deters crime, adultery, urinating in public and other civil menaces. It also, naturally, stops people who are different to the norm expressing that difference, so there is a fine line between encouraging people to be nicer and fascism.

Do say 'Social media lynch mobs are an extension of humanity's need to force conformity on others, often at the expense of free speech and reasonableness.'

Don't say 'I HOPE YOU DIE AND CATS EAT UR BRAINS.'

And if anyone tells you that modern-day lynch mobs aren't as bad as the ones that used to hang people for no reason, feel free to remind them of the words of Clarence Thomas, one of the first African-Americans to become a justice of the US Supreme Court.

Recalling his childhood in Georgia, he said: 'I'd grown up fearing the lynch mobs of the Ku Klux Klan; as an adult I was starting to wonder if I'd been afraid of the wrong white people all along – where I was being pursued not by bigots in white robes, but by left-wing zealots draped in flowing sanctimony.'

—— *ℬ* ——

'To live is to war with trolls.'

Henrik Ibsen

ANTI-SOCIAL MEDIA

With every technological innovation, there are people who use it to be as unkind as possible to other human beings, which makes them afraid of it.

This is why newspapers like reports about how this newfangled computer business leads to stalking, murders, bad grammar, porn everywhere you look, socialism, and anything else that might give traditional newspaper readers a headache.

But what they fail to point out in every article entitled 'Is Twitter the End of Civilisation?' is that pretty much the same fear arose with the telephone, bicycles, motor cars, nuclear power and the discovery of fire.

First caveman 'Behold, I've made fire!'

Second caveman 'Great, let's sit around it and feel warm and have a chat.'

Third caveman 'I've burned my finger. Bloody fire.'

Fourth caveman 'Let's use it to burn the village next door.'

Fifth caveman 'I'm starting #PutOutTheFlames.'

First caveman 'Oh, for God's sake.'

Social media can be a force for bad as well as good. Sometimes this is down to stupidity, occasionally it's due to mental illness, and now and again it's actually planned that way.

Let's start with the stupids, which all too often involves someone with a job title like 'Creative Brand Engineer' who tells a corporate client that what they really need to make their product sell is a hashtag.

WHEN HASHTAGS GO WRONG

For a prime example, we need look no further than McDonald's, which paid a tweeting service to promote its hashtags so that it could be top of Twitter's trending topics – the list of the most talked-about subjects on the website.

The social media team tweeted about recognising the efforts of its hard-working staff using the hashtag #McDstories, in the hope that this would show customers how much work goes into a burger and fries.

At first, it worked. Or it worked if you're not one to object to lazy spelling. A potato supplier, for example, tweeted: 'When u make something w/ pride, people can taste it.'

But very quickly, critics jumped on the hashtag to describe dining horror stories, accusing McDonald's of making them sick, and flouting animal welfare rules. One user even said they got a Big Mac with a human fingernail in it.

Before long, the benighted tweeting service was involved in a long debate with animal rights group PETA, which accused them of using mechanically separated chicken for its McNuggets, which the firm denied.

McDonald's rapidly abandoned the whole thing. Rick Wion, the firm's social media director, said: 'Within an hour we saw that it wasn't going as planned. It was negative enough that we set about a change of course.'

THINGS NOT TO DO

So there was really no excuse two years later when the New York Police Department decided one quiet afternoon to get people to tweet pictures taken with some of the Big Apple's finest. 'You might be on our Facebook page!' was the tempting offer.

Cue a deluge of pictures of alleged police brutality, including Occupy Wall Street protesters being dragged off in cuffs, an 84-year-old man arrested for jaywalking and even of one officer frisking a dog.

By midnight, there were 70,000 tweets on #myNYPD alleging police brutality and naming victims of police shootings, and more were being posted at the rate of 10,000 an hour.

It even sparked a similar trend in Los Angeles for #myLAPD, who hadn't even started it.

Equally dense was the public relations bunny who came up with the wheeze for an executive at Wall Street bank JP Morgan, at the time involved in allegations of mis-selling and heavy trading losses, to answer people's questions on Twitter using the hashtag #askJPM.

In what became known as a 'snarkpocalypse', the poor man was subjected to 8,000 questions a minute including 'Quick! You're in a room with no key, a chair, two paper clips, and a light bulb. How do you defraud investors?', 'Is it easier to purchase a congressional representative or a senator?' and 'Why is it when the poor commit crimes we need more cops and mandatory sentences and when the rich commit crimes we need deregulation?'

He didn't answer them, which is a shame, because the whole Q&A was cancelled.

British Gas made a similar boo-boo with #AskBG – 'My office has a window where the sun comes in and makes the side of my head really hot. How much do I owe you?' – and the bosses of record store HMV must have regretted ever getting a corporate Twitter account when an antsy member of staff live-tweeted the mass firing of 190 employees.

Gems included 'We're tweeting live from HR where we're all being fired! Exciting!!!' and 'Just overheard our Marketing Director (he's staying, folks!) ask "How do I shut down Twitter?"'

But by far the worst corporate promotion exercise, and one every bluffer needs to remember, was when Simon Cowell's record company decided to promote its star Susan Boyle's new album.

Her Twitter feed (not operated by Susan) invited followers to a 'listening party' at which Susan herself would answer questions from fans.

Unfortunately, the hashtag they settled on was #susanalbumparty.

BLUFFER'S TIP *When attempting to subvert a corporate hashtag for good, remember that it takes skill, wit and knowledge.*

For example, when social media users realised tweets hashtagged #makemesmile were being automatically streamed unedited on the Vodafone UK website, they were able to use that knowledge to publish allegations of corporate tax avoidance, which is also skilful and witty.

And finally, if you have a grudge, you might need to use what's known as 'complaintvertising'.

When Chicago hairdresser Hasan Syed flew business class to Paris on British Airways, the airline lost his luggage and failed to respond to his complaints. So he spent $1,000 to buy a promoted tweet that appeared automatically at the top of pages, saying: 'Don't fly @ British_Airways. Their customer service is horrendous.'

It was seen by 50,000 people on both sides of the Atlantic. Expensive, but satisfying.

WHEN IN TROUBLE, BLAME SOCIAL MEDIA

Celebrities adore social media, not least because it's all me, me, me, and it's filled with people telling them they're wonderful. They also get to immediately correct inaccurate press reports and can rustle up some tabloid headlines just for saying something silly/libellous/offensive.

These delicate flowers find it difficult to put up with criticism though, and tend to flounce off social media whenever things get sticky. The good bluffer needs to know not just who the quitters are, but how often they come slinking back…

Stephen Fry threatened to leave Twitter in 2010 after another user called him 'a bit…boring'. Fry announced 'I retire from Twitter henceforward. Bye everyone.' Cue thousands of people saying 'Oh no, please don't,' and Fry sheepishly returned. A few months later he tweeted 'Bye bye' again after an interviewer reported he had claimed women don't enjoy sex. He flounced off again in 2016 after a backlash about a BAFTAs remark. He came back. He can't stay away.

In 2009 **Miley Cyrus** made a rap video about quitting social media saying she wanted to 'keep my private life private'. She returned 17 months later, and now has 38.5 million followers on Twitter and 73.6 million on Instagram. How private can you get?

30 Rock star **Alec Baldwin** left Twitter in 2011 after he was thrown off an American Airlines plane for allegedly playing an iPhone game. He came back, and quit again in 2013 after his wife was wrongly criticised by a journalist for tweeting during a funeral. He returned and in 2017 announced another departure following unwise remarks over the Hollywood sex abuse scandal.

Lady Gaga took a vow of social media silence to raise awareness of World AIDS Day. She went silent. No one minded. Then she came back again. Phew, that showed AIDS!

William Shatner, AKA Captain Kirk, announced in 2014 that, after long deliberation, he was leaving Twitter. The next day he tweeted: 'Made a bad midnight decision. Pressured by too many things on my plate. In a pique, I quit Twitter. Boy did I make a mistake.'

BLUFFER'S TIP *They come back. They always do.*

HOW TO SPOT A TROLL

The bluffer needs to be aware that social media, like everything else in human society, has its anti-social elements. In the world of the Internet, as previously noted, these have become known by the catch-all term of 'trolls'.

However, not all trolls are really trolls. Some trolling isn't trolling at all, and there are some easy guidelines for dealing with other people online which should ensure that, if you troll anyone, you at least know how to do it properly.

So how do you spot one?

1. **True trolls are Internet users who set out to ruin someone else's day.** Everyone else is merely someone who disagrees with you, which is allowed. It is hard to differentiate between someone who is 'generally disagreeable to the

entire world' and 'currently disagreeing with me'. So we move to...

2. **They can't speak proper, innit.** Their punctuation, spelling or grammar is so far round the spout it's actually random. Of course, this could also indicate someone with a learning difficulty, so to be kind we need to check off some more identifying factors such as...

3. **They say extremely unreasonable things.** Not just 'Yeah well, so what, copper?' but posting on the Facebook memorial pages of murdered children that they deserved it, searching out women to call them whores, or sending rape and death threats. This isn't normal debate.

4. **They are not friends with logic.** If you question them, ask them why or suggest substantiating this or that, they will scream, kick a table or call you a Nazi.

5. **The sheer volume of their posts – either in word count or frequency – indicates a serious personality disorder.**

6. **If you saw them on the bus, you would sit elsewhere.**

That's your genuine troll – someone who probably would be living under a bridge eating rodents and, despite their hateful outpourings would, if we could see them, have our sympathy.

HOWEVER – this is too reasonable to relate to the Internet. Publishing in real life involves lots of people and lawyers and effort, whereas doing it online merely requires two fingers and the wish to stick them up at someone.

Social media, just like any other kind of gossip, forces conformity. If you step out of line, if you wear the wrong clothes or think the wrong thing, someone will have a go at you. Everyone seems to be a troll in one way or another; it's almost a badge of honour.

Do say If you've been online for five minutes and no one's said you're a troll, then you're probably a spambot.

Don't say What's a spambot?

HOW TO BE A (GOOD) TROLL

The Internet's prime purpose is to facilitate uniformity of thought (always a good starting point for the bluffer when discussing social media). The rules for what you're allowed to think online change all the time, but they're usually something like this:

1. Julian Assange is the victim of a CIA and media conspiracy aimed at causing his eventual death.

2. Rupert Murdoch is Satan.

3. You are compelled to say RIP about the death of strangers.

4. You are not allowed to offend anyone, ever.

5. Anything someone else says can be taken as offensive.

6. Being offensive is illegal.

7. Cats do the cutest things.

But in the land of the bland, the interestingly different is king. Shouting wildly about stuff in ways that make no sense can confer celebrity, attention and validity, which is why people do it.

So if you want to stand out from the crowd and revel in being a troll, you need to break those rules good and hard:

1. Pick fights with celebrities for a laugh.

2. If you can get them to flounce off Twitter while you're at it, this is a double-win.

3. Announce you hate cats.

4. Say 'Actually, I quite admire Rupert Murdoch.'

5. Invoke Godwin's Law (*see* 'Glossary') as soon as possible in any debate. This is the observation that 'As an Internet discussion grows longer, the probability

of a comparison with Nazis or Hitler approaches one.'
Do what you can to make this happen sooner.

6. Call a stranger a troll, or a prostitute, a conspirator, a liar, a spy, a Communist or a Nazi even if you don't know them, their pimp, or their MI6 handler. Do it all in under 30 seconds and you get a special gold star.

HOW TO HANDLE TROLLS

1. Develop a thick skin.

2. Then develop an EVEN THICKER one.

3. Avoid the mentally ill unless you're qualified to deal with them.

4. Remember this is supposed to be fun.

5. If you want the Internet to agree with you, it is time to switch it off and go outside for some fresh air.

6. Name, shame, retweet them and correct their posts for spelling and grammar. This usually shuts them up.

Don't forget the Web is barely 30 years old, Facebook hasn't hit puberty yet and Twitter is still at primary school. There are a lot of cavemen out there, and it's tricky to get their heads around all this stuff.

So if you want to survive it, the basic rule of thumb is to behave online in exactly the same way you would at a bus stop – keep the swearing down, avoid the weirdos, be nice to old ladies, that sort of thing.

And the final rule for handling trolls is to put up with whatever you'd put up with at the bus stop, and not an insult more. Laugh at them, block them, report it to the driver, and only call the police *in extremis*.

Do say 'If we only let people we agree with on the Internet, it'd be empty.'

Don't say 'I thought trolls only existed in Norse mythology.'

SOCIAL MEDIA AND SUICIDE

In 2008 UK police warned that social media might actively encourage suicide through glamorising the dead, Facebook memorials, and peer pressure. Senior church figures have warned that the transient nature of online friendships can cause real-world angst when they collapse.

More often than not, the suicides that draw attention are those of teenagers. Dozens of pro-suicide websites and forums exist, offering advice on how to go about it and how to buy stuff online to help you do it. Opinion is divided about whether these suicides would happen anyway or if social media somehow encourages them.

In 2008 it was reported Abraham Biggs, 19, had posted online he was going to kill himself and invited people to watch a live videocast. Around 1,500 people signed up to watch, posted insults, and told him to get on with it. Those monitoring the site presumed it was a joke. It wasn't, and police discovered his body in his bedroom in Miami.

In 2013 Hannah Smith, 14, was found hanging in her bedroom. She had complained of being bullied on anonymous site Ask.fm. After her death, an investigation found Hannah had sent the anonymous messages to herself.

People post suicide notes online, make pleas for help online, get bullied online and, as with many things on social media, the actions seem distant and aren't taken seriously.

There are also social media forums set up to help those who feel suicidal – they're right there on Google, next to the ones telling people to hurry up and die already.

Humans, eh? Odd bunch.

'It is not in the stars to hold our destiny but in ourselves.'

William Shakespeare

INTO THE UNKNOWN

If you've made it this far, then you're now officially an expert in social media. You might not actually have a Twitter or Facebook account, but you could certainly bluff your way through a TV interview on the topic while sounding like an expert, which is about as close as any of us can get.

But what of social media itself? What is going to happen in the future with all this information and emotion buzzing around the Internet?

THE BAD POSSIBILITIES

Some people think social media is already dying out. The rapid popularity of social networks is so similar to the dynamics of an infectious disease that some spods at Princeton University reckon it's about to start declining.

Because people join social networks when their friends do, there comes a point when everyone's already on it. The researchers say we've hit peak-Facebook already. In 2014 the site was predicted to lose 80 per cent of its 1.2 billion users by 2017. In 2017, it had 2.1 billion accounts, which just shows how difficult it is to predict anything in this bizarre new world.

Facebook is suffering from a reputation for selling user data. It also has privacy issues, and you can't avoid the fact it's been around so long in Internet terms that your boss AND your mum are on it which makes it 75 per cent less fun.

If a newer, better, less irritating social network comes along, Facebook could well go the way of Friends Reunited and become more of a cobwebsite. (Geddit?)

Perhaps it's already started for Twitter: In early 2014 the site announced a £395 million loss and an estimated £6 billion was wiped off its shares in a day after it admitted the rate of sign-up was tailing off. In 2016 it was reckoned to be worth $10 billion, which is a lot. It was previously valued at $50 billion.

Therein is the risk of investing in social media, be it by running your business through it, putting your whole life online or buying shares. There will, almost certainly, come a point that you wish you hadn't.

But while some of us might want to pull back from social media, others are going to throw themselves at it like lemmings that've found a new and exciting cliff.

For example, there's Michelle Chapman who was jailed for 20 months for setting up Facebook profiles in the name of her dad and stepmother then using them to send herself abusive messages. She reported it to the police, who first arrested her stepmother and cautioned her dad before realising who the culprit was.

Then there's Chris Sevier of Florida, who launched a

legal battle in a bid to marry his laptop. He says he's in love with his MacBook and claims that by being denied a marriage licence he's being discriminated against. He failed, but later claimed to have married it anyway in New Mexico.

Lastly there's the cautionary case of beauty salon receptionist Gemma Worrall, who tweeted 'if barraco barner is our president why is he getting involved with Russia, scary' and was cyberbullied by thousands of people for not knowing how to spell Barack Obama or realising that, as she's British, he's not her president.

People will almost certainly be more guarded on social media, aware of the possibilities of being mocked/arrested/fired for saying the wrong thing.

And with new, wearable tech like camera glasses and tweeting wristwatches, it'll be possible for stalkers to take your picture and upload it without you even knowing what they were up to.

But it might not be all bad.

THE GOOD POSSIBILITIES

The rapid spread of information on social media – even if it is only about why your lunchtime sandwich was below par – makes the world a better place.

Got a complaint about your bank or gas supplier? Tweet about it. All major firms now have a social media team whose job it is to find and resolve complaints, and it can be a lot quicker than trying to do it the traditional way.

Let's not forget those who've used social media for good. People like the late teenaged cancer sufferer

Stephen Sutton, whose blogging and tweeting helped to raise £5.5 million for charity; the Amsterdam teachers who set up Facebook timelines to teach pupils in real time about Magellan's voyage to the Americas; charities who use it to raise money; and awareness projects like @everydaysexism who campaign to make people more thoughtful.

Social media has been used by millions of pet owners to find lost and stolen animals – just think of all those tearful children who got Kitty back.

Research from the University of California (where else?) analysed a billion Facebook status updates over three years and found positive ones produced more responses and spread further than negative ones – smile on Facebook, and happiness multiplies.

Kobe City University in Japan found that in countries where social media is heavily used, there are lower suicide rates and higher self-esteem. Countries whose people don't tweet much are 'less emotionally expressive', it found.

An American project that followed silver surfers found that elderly people who spend time online are less likely to have depression and feelings of isolation and loneliness.

Social media is giving rise to new words all the time. In 2014 the word 'adorkable', meaning someone geeky but attractive and first coined on Twitter in 2007, was added to the Collins English Dictionary.

And surgeons have started using Google Glass, a new bit of kit with a camera and live Internet feed loaded onto what looks like a pair of spectacles, in the operating theatre to give medical students a perfect view of medical procedures.

It could one day be used to teach new doctors in the developing world, or to relay procedures by a junior surgeon to a senior one in a different city or country for advice.

Meanwhile, as you waste time on Instagram or Pinterest, they're being used by others to share research, ideas, helpful tips and even democracy protests. China has an army of Internet censors who patrol the Web and block anything deemed offensive by the Communist authorities, but it is not watertight. Stuff leaks through, news and tragedies are shared, and not every tyrant or absolute ruler can keep all social media at bay.

Hopefully by now you know what social media is, who uses it, and all the many weird and wonderful things they use it for – from finding fame to getting laid, trolling to getting arrested, and how not to get into trouble when you're doing all those things.

But the most important thing any bluffer needs to know when asked about the future of social media is that it is going to be whatever all the people who use it want it to be. Social media boils down to a group of humans doing what they always have done – being nice and nasty to one another, making money, finding love, causing offence and having a laugh.

As social media spreads its net ever more widely, as a planet and a species we'll have more democracy, more rapidly inflated scandals, more baby-faced billionaires.

And many millions more cat videos. It seems there's nothing we can do about that.

If you want to sum up social media in 140 characters – just the right length for a status update, tweet or picture caption – it'd be something like this:

Social media (n) The latest method humans have devised for acting like arses most of the time. Occasionally nice things can happen too.

GLOSSARY

AFAIK 'As far as I know'. An acronym used to create plausible deniability for the inaccuracy of whatever it was you just posted.

Asterisks Placed around a word to indicate emphasis or sarcasm, like you didn't know *that* already.

Bitly Website providing shortened versions of website urls, making it easier for people who can't shorten what they say to post, and now used as a verb by people who should be shot. 'Can't you bitly that?'

CD9 Code 9, parents are around.

Dweet Drunk tweeting, which is hysterical if it's not you making a habit of it.

FTW 'For the win', an initialism from social media's gaming past indicating someone or something should be victorious in an entirely fictional and unimportant way.

FYI 'For your information', only used by passive-aggressive pedants.

GIF A picture that moves and is on a short loop, enabling people to see a cat falling into a bucket of water AGAIN and AGAIN.

Godwin's Law Named after US attorney Mike Godwin who came up with the rule that any Internet argument will eventually involve one person invoking the Nazis. Used mainly, it must be said, by the person who just lost the argument, e.g., 'I think we should burn all books,' 'OMG that's what the Nazis said,' 'HA! Godwin's Law! I win!'

Hashtags A way of tagging a post, tweet or picture in a particular category. To get it seen by more people, use a popular hashtag. To be funny, invent one of your own.

H/T Hat tip, a way of attributing a statement to another user.

IRL 'In real life', where there are no computers and people talk to one another and there's fresh air and sunshine.

Linking Generally considered polite to substantiate what you're saying by including a link to the web page with the information under discussion. Has the happy effect of letting the original author take the flak if it's wrong.

Livetweeting Tweeting something as it happens, for example your train journey. 'ZOMG! No crisps on the food trolley! #starvingtodeath.'

LOL If you are young, this means 'laugh out loud' and is used at the end of a post to indicate humour. If you are over 50, or a prime minister, it means 'lots of love' and is used to show you like the person you're talking to, who will be too touched to explain you've got it wrong.

LOLZ An infinite amount of whatever you think LOL means.

Nazis They're everywhere.

OMG 'Oh my God', used to indicate mild shock.

OMFG An even more emphatic indication of shock.

Pwned Another piece of gaming slang from when the Internet was young. Is supposed to be 'owned', to indicate someone has been utterly beaten, but a fat-fingered programmer mistyped it and now it's a word all by itself.

ROFL 'Rolling on the floor laughing', for times when LOL just isn't funny enough.

ROFLCOPTER Rolling on the floor laughing and thrashing my limbs about in the style of a helicopter's rotor blades, for when you are being intensely sarcastic.

RT A retweet, when someone has shared whatever was tweeted without comment.

Selfie Taking a picture of yourself and posting it online, usually with a 'duck face' and your upper lip stuck out.

Shelfie Taking a picture of your shelf and posting it online, thereby mocking others' personal vanity with evidence of your books/knick-knacks/porn collection.

STFU Shut the f*** up.

Streisand Effect The process whereby complaining about something online makes it a billion times more noticeable.

Tweeple People of Twitter.

Vaguebooking Updating your status with something meaningless as a way of getting attention.

YOLO You only live once, unless you're 007 or a cat.

ZOMG A sarcastic comment on an overenthusiastic poster.

A BIT MORE BLUFFING...

Bluffer's® GUIDE TO BREXIT

Bluffer's® GUIDE TO CRICKET

Bluffer's® GUIDE TO MANAGEMENT

Bluffer's® GUIDE TO CYCLING

Bluffer's® GUIDE TO SOCIAL MEDIA

Bluffer's® GUIDE TO ETIQUETTE

Bluffer's® GUIDE TO RACING

Bluffer's® GUIDE TO GOLF

Bluffer's® GUIDE TO WINE

Bluffer's® GUIDE TO JAZZ

Bluffer's® GUIDE TO DOGS

Bluffer's® GUIDE TO FISHING

Bluffer's® GUIDE TO OPERA

Bluffer's® GUIDE TO CHOCOLATE

Bluffer's® GUIDE TO CATS

Bluffer's® GUIDE TO BEER

Available from all good bookshops

bluffers.com